# Lua Simplified

A Beginner's Guide to Powerful Scripting

Gabriel Kroenenn

# Contents

## 8   Mastering Text                          80

## 9   Handling the Unexpected                93

## 10   Organizing Your Code                  102

# 1

# Your Lua Adventure Begins

Imagine a programming language that's small, fast, and surprisingly simple, yet capable enough to power parts of massive online games, web servers handling millions of requests, and even help artists create stunning visuals. That language is Lua! Think of it not as a heavy industrial machine, but more like a sharp, adaptable toolkit, perfect for adding scripting capabilities to bigger projects or for building nimble applications from scratch. This chapter is your starting point. We'll uncover what makes Lua tick, peek into its interesting origins, see where it's making a difference in the world, and importantly, get your own computer ready to speak Lua. Your journey into this elegant language starts right here.

## What Makes Lua Sparkle?

So, what's the big deal about Lua? Why choose it over the many other languages out there? Lua has a few core ideas that make it stand out.

First, it's incredibly **lightweight**. The entire Lua interpreter (the program that runs your Lua code) is tiny, measured in kilobytes, not megabytes. This makes it fantastic for situations where resources are limited, like in mobile games or embedded systems (think smart devices or controllers). It doesn't demand a lot from your computer.

Second, Lua is **fast**. For a language that's interpreted (read and executed on the fly, rather than compiled to machine code beforehand), Lua performs remarkably well. Its simple design allows for efficient execution, often rivaling or even surpassing other scripting languages in speed tests. This performance is a key reason it's chosen for demanding tasks like game logic.

Third, Lua was designed from the ground up to be **embeddable**. This means it's easy to integrate Lua *into* applications written in other languages, typically C or C++. An application can use Lua to allow users to write scripts, customize behavior, or rapidly prototype features without touching the core C/C++ code. It acts like a controllable extension mechanism.

Beyond these technical points, Lua embraces:

- **Simplicity:** Lua has a relatively small set of core concepts. Its syntax is clean and avoids unnecessary clutter. This makes it easier to learn and read than many other languages. You won't find dozens of ways to do the same thing; usually, there's one clear, idiomatic way.
- **Portability:** Lua is written in clean ANSI C, meaning it can run on virtually any platform that has a C compiler. From massive mainframes to tiny micro-controllers, Windows, macOS, Linux, mobile operating systems – Lua feels at home almost anywhere.
- **Flexibility:** Despite its simplicity, Lua provides powerful mechanisms for creating complex structures. Its single data-structuring tool, the **table** (which we'll explore thoroughly in Chapter 6), can be used to create arrays, dictionaries, objects, and more. This flexibility allows you to adapt the language to your specific needs.

These characteristics combine to make Lua a pragmatic choice for a wide range of problems.

# A Glimpse into Lua's Past

Every language has a story, and Lua's is quite interesting. It didn't emerge from a large corporation or a purely academic setting. Lua was born in Brazil in 1993 at the Pontifical Catholic University of Rio de Janeiro (PUC-Rio).

Its creators – Roberto Ierusalimschy, Luiz Henrique de Figueiredo, and Waldemar Celes – were working within Tecgraf, the Computer Graphics Technology Group, which had close ties to Petrobras, the Brazilian oil giant. Petrobras needed ways to configure complex engineering software and allow engineers (who weren't necessarily expert programmers) to customize simulations and data analysis tasks.

At the time, there wasn't a perfect solution. Existing scripting languages were often too complex, not easily portable across the different systems Petrobras used, or had restrictive licenses. They needed something simple, portable, and easily embeddable into their existing C applications. Finding nothing suitable, they decided to create their own language.

They combined ideas from earlier languages they had developed (DEL and Sol) and focused intently on the goals of simplicity, portability, and embeddability. The name "Lua" means "Moon" in Portuguese, a fitting name for a language born from the earlier "Sol" (Sun). Lua was designed to solve real-world problems from day one, and this practical origin continues to shape its philosophy.

# Lua in the Wild

Despite its relatively low profile compared to giants like Python or JavaScript, Lua is used in some very high-profile and demanding environments. You've likely encountered Lua without even realizing it!

- **Game Development:** This is arguably Lua's most famous domain. Its speed, small footprint, and ease of embedding make it ideal for scripting game logic, character AI, user interfaces, and event handling.
    - **Roblox:** Uses Luau, a dialect of Lua, as its primary scripting language, empowering millions of users to create their own games and experiences.
    - **World of Warcraft:** Allows players to extensively customize their user interface using Lua addons.
    - **Defold Engine, LÖVE (Love2D), Corona SDK (now Solar2D):** Popular game frameworks built heavily around Lua.
    - Countless others, from indie hits to AAA titles like *Civilization*, often use Lua for scripting tasks.
- **Web Servers and Infrastructure:** While less common for general web development, Lua excels in high-performance scenarios.
    - **OpenResty:** A powerful web platform built on Nginx that integrates Lua extensively. It allows developers to write highly efficient web applications, APIs, and gateways directly in Lua. Many high-traffic websites use OpenResty/Lua to handle requests efficiently.

- **Kong:** An popular open-source API gateway built on OpenResty.
- **Redis:** Allows scripting database interactions using Lua for atomic operations.
- **Application Extension:** Many desktop applications use Lua as an internal scripting engine.
    - **Adobe Lightroom:** Uses Lua for developing plugins and automating tasks.
    - **Neovim / Vim:** Modern text editors that allow extensive customization via Lua.
    - **Wireshark:** The network protocol analyzer uses Lua for writing dissectors and taps.
- **Embedded Systems:** Its small size makes Lua suitable for devices where memory and processing power are limited, although C remains dominant here.

This is just a sample! Lua pops up wherever there's a need for a fast, lightweight, and easily embeddable scripting language. Its pragmatic design has earned it a dedicated following in these niches.

# Setting Up Your Lua Playground

Enough talk, let's get Lua running on your machine! Thankfully, this is usually a straightforward process.

## Getting Lua

How you install Lua depends on your operating system:

- **Linux:** Lua is often available through your distribution's package manager.
    - On Debian/Ubuntu: `sudo apt update && sudo apt install lua5.4` (or `lua5.3`, `lua5.2`, `lua5.1` depending on availability and preference – we'll focus on modern Lua, but concepts are similar).
    - On Fedora: `sudo dnf install lua`
    - On Arch: `sudo pacman -S lua`
- **macOS:** The easiest way is often using a package manager like Homebrew.
    - With Homebrew: `brew install lua`
- **Windows:** You have a few options:
    - **Lua Binaries:** You can download pre-compiled Windows binaries directly from the LuaBinaries project (often found via a web search for

"Lua Binaries download"). Download the package, unzip it, and you'll find `lua5x.exe` (e.g., `lua54.exe`). It's helpful to add the directory containing this executable to your system's PATH environment variable so you can run it from any command prompt.

- **Scoop:** If you use the Scoop command-line installer for Windows: `scoop install lua`
- **WSL (Windows Subsystem for Linux):** If you have WSL set up, you can follow the Linux instructions within your WSL environment.

To check if Lua is installed and accessible from your terminal or command prompt, simply type:

```
lua -v
```

If it's installed correctly, you should see something like:

```
Lua 5.4.6 Copyright (C) 1994-2023 Lua.org, PUC-Rio
```

*(The exact version number might differ, which is usually fine for learning.)* If you get an error like "command not found," double-check your installation steps and ensure Lua's location is in your system's PATH.

## Meeting the Lua Interpreter

The simplest way to interact with Lua is through its interactive interpreter. Just type `lua` in your terminal or command prompt and press Enter:

```
lua
```

You'll see the Lua version information again, followed by a prompt, usually a single greater-than sign (>):

```
Lua 5.4.6 Copyright (C) 1994-2023 Lua.org, PUC-Rio
> _
```

Now you can type Lua commands directly, and Lua will execute them immediately. Let's try the traditional first program:

```
> print("Hello from the interpreter!")
```

Press Enter, and Lua responds:

```
Hello from the interpreter!
>_
```

The `print` function simply displays whatever you give it (in this case, the text string `"Hello from the interpreter!"`). We'll use `print` a lot for seeing results.

You can also do quick calculations:

```
> 2 + 2
```

Output:

```
4
>_
```

To exit the interactive interpreter, you can usually type `os.exit()` or press `Ctrl+Z` then Enter on Windows, or `Ctrl+D` on Linux/macOS.

```
> os.exit()
```

The interactive mode is great for trying out small snippets of code or exploring how functions work.

## Running Lua Scripts from Files

While the interpreter is handy for quick tests, most real programs are written in files, often called scripts. Let's create one.

1. Open a plain text editor (like Notepad on Windows, TextEdit on macOS - in plain text mode!, gedit on Linux, VS Code, Sublime Text, etc.). **Do not use** a word processor like Microsoft Word, as they add extra formatting.

2. Type the following line into the editor:

   ```
   print("Hello from my first Lua script!")
   ```

3. Save the file with a `.lua` extension. Let's call it `hello.lua`. Make sure you know which directory you saved it in.

4. Open your terminal or command prompt again.

5. Navigate to the directory where you saved `hello.lua`. You use the `cd` (change directory) command for this. For example, if you saved it in a `LuaProjects` folder on your Desktop:

   - Linux/macOS: `cd ~/Desktop/LuaProjects`
   - Windows: `cd %USERPROFILE%\Desktop\LuaProjects` (Adjust the path as needed!)

6. Now, tell the Lua interpreter to execute the script file:

```
lua hello.lua
```

Lua will run the code inside the file, and you should see the output:

```
Hello from my first Lua script!
```

You've just written and executed your first Lua script! This process – writing code in a `.lua` file and running it with the `lua` command – is how you'll develop most of your Lua programs.

# Chapter Summary

In this chapter, we've unveiled the essence of Lua – its lightweight nature, speed, and embeddability, coupled with a philosophy of simplicity and portability. We journeyed back to its practical origins in Brazil and saw its widespread use, especially in game development and high-performance web systems. Most importantly, you've successfully set up your Lua environment and interacted with it both through the interpreter and by running your very first script file.

You now have the basic tools and context. In the next chapter, we'll start building your Lua vocabulary, learning how to store information using variables and understanding the fundamental data types that form the building blocks of any Lua program. Let's start talking to the computer!

# 2
# Talking to Your Computer in Lua

Alright, you've successfully set up your Lua environment in Chapter 1 and proven you can run Lua code. Now, it's time to learn the actual language – the words and grammar Lua understands. Think of it like learning the basic sentence structure before you can write a story. In this chapter, we'll cover the essential rules for writing Lua statements, how to create containers called **variables** to hold information, and the different kinds of information, or **data types**, that Lua can work with. We'll also revisit the print function you met briefly, as it's our primary way to see what our code is doing.

## The Basic Rules of Lua Conversation

Every language, human or computer, has rules about how sentences (or *statements*, in programming terms) are formed. Lua's rules are designed to be simple and flexible.

### Writing Code

Lua executes code one statement at a time, usually one statement per line. A simple statement might be assigning a value to a variable or calling a function.

```
-- This is a statement that prints text
```

```
print("One statement per line is common")

-- This is another statement assigning a value
local message = "Hello again!"
```

You *can* put multiple statements on a single line by separating them with a semicolon (;), but this is **not** common practice in Lua and generally makes code harder to read.

```
local x = 10; print(x) -- Works, but less readable
```

Most Lua programmers stick to one statement per line for clarity. Semicolons are almost always optional at the end of a line.

One crucial rule: Lua is **case-sensitive**. This means myVariable is completely different from myvariable or MyVariable. Be consistent with your capitalization! print works, but Print or PRINT will cause an error.

## Making Notes

Sometimes, you want to leave notes in your code for yourself or other programmers. These notes, called **comments**, are ignored by the Lua interpreter. They are purely for human readers.

Lua has two ways to write comments:

1. **Single-line comments:** Start with two hyphens (--). Everything from the -- to the end of the line is ignored.

   ```
   -- This entire line is a comment.
   local score = 100 -- This part is a comment explaining the score.
   ```

2. **Multi-line comments:** Start with --[[ and end with ]]. Everything between these markers is ignored, even across multiple lines. This is useful for commenting out larger blocks of code temporarily or writing longer explanations.

   ```
   --[[
   This is a multi-line comment.
   It can span several lines and is useful
   for longer descriptions or temporarily
   disabling a section of code.
   local old_code = "don't run this now"
   ]]
   ```

```
print("This line will run.")
```

*A common trick:* To quickly disable a multi-line comment block, just add an extra hyphen at the beginning: `---[[ ... ]]`. Now the first line is a single-line comment, and the block is no longer seen as a multi-line comment by Lua. Remove the extra hyphen to re-enable it.

## Whitespace and Readability

Whitespace refers to spaces, tabs, and blank lines. Lua is quite flexible about whitespace *between* elements in your code. `local x=10` works the same as `local x = 10`.

However, whitespace *within* names or keywords is obviously not allowed (`localx` is not the same as `local x`).

More importantly, **use whitespace consistently** to make your code readable. Indenting code blocks (like those inside loops or `if` statements, which we'll see in Chapter 4) makes the structure clear. Blank lines can separate logical chunks of code. While Lua doesn't *force* indentation, readable code is maintainable code. Most Lua code uses spaces (typically 2 or 4) for indentation.

# Storing Information

Imagine you're baking. You use bowls to hold ingredients like flour or sugar temporarily. In programming, you use **variables** to hold pieces of information, like a player's score, a user's name, or the result of a calculation.

## What are Variables?

A variable is essentially a named storage location in the computer's memory. You give it a name (a label for the box) and put some data inside it. Later, you can use the name to retrieve the data or put different data into the box.

## Creating Variables

You create (or *declare*) a variable and give it its initial value using an **assignment statement**, which uses the equals sign (=):

```lua
local playerName = "Alice"
local currentScore = 0
local speed = 5.5
local isGameOver = false
```

Let's break this down:

- `local`: This keyword is highly recommended! It declares the variable as **local**, meaning it's only accessible within the current block of code (like the current file, or inside a function - more on scope in Chapter 5). Using `local` helps prevent accidentally overwriting variables used elsewhere and is generally good practice. If you omit `local`, the variable becomes **global**, accessible everywhere, which can lead to messy code and hard-to-find bugs in larger projects. **Always use `local` unless you have a specific reason not to.**
- `playerName`, `currentScore`, `speed`, `isGameOver`: These are the **variable names** (the labels on our boxes).
- `=`: This is the **assignment operator**. It takes the value on the right and stores it in the variable on the left. It does *not* mean "is equal to" in a mathematical sense (that's `==`, which we'll see in Chapter 3).
- `"Alice"`, `0`, `5.5`, `false`: These are the **values** being stored in the variables. They represent different kinds of data.

You can change the value stored in a variable later by assigning a new value to it:

```lua
local currentScore = 0
print(currentScore) -- Output: 0

currentScore = 100 -- Assign a new value
print(currentScore) -- Output: 100

currentScore = currentScore + 50 -- Use the current value in a calculation
print(currentScore) -- Output: 150
```

# Naming Rules and Good Habits

Choosing good variable names is important for readability. Lua has rules for what constitutes a valid name:

- Names can consist of letters (a-z, A-Z), numbers (0-9), and underscores (_).
- Names **cannot** start with a number.
- Names are **case-sensitive** (`score` is different from `Score`).

- Certain words, called **keywords** or **reserved words**, have special meaning in Lua and cannot be used as variable names (e.g., `local`, `function`, `if`, `then`, `end`, `while`, `for`, `nil`, `true`, `false`). Your text editor might highlight these words differently.

Good habits for naming:

- Choose descriptive names: `player_score` is better than `ps` or `x`.
- Be consistent: If you use `camelCase` (like `playerName`), use it everywhere. If you prefer `snake_case` (like `player_name`), stick with that. Both are common in the Lua world.
- Avoid excessively long names, but clarity is more important than brevity.

# Lua's Building Blocks

Variables store data, but what *kind* of data can they store? Lua has a set of fundamental **data types**. Every value in Lua belongs to one of these types. Lua is a **dynamically typed** language, which means you don't have to declare the type of a variable beforehand; the type is determined by the value it currently holds. A variable can hold a number at one moment and a string the next.

Lua has eight basic types:

1. `nil`: This type has only one value: `nil`. It represents the absence of a useful value. It's often used to indicate "nothing" or "empty." Variables that haven't been assigned a value yet will have the value `nil`. Assigning `nil` to a variable is also how you can effectively delete it (making it available for garbage collection, see Chapter 13).

   ```
   local emptyVariable -- This variable holds nil initially
   print(emptyVariable) -- Output: nil
   emptyVariable = nil -- Explicitly setting it to nil
   ```

2. `boolean`: This type represents logical values and has only two possible values: `true` and `false`. Booleans are essential for making decisions in your code (using `if` statements, Chapter 4). Note that they are keywords and must be lowercase.

   ```
   local isReady = true
   local hasFailed = false
   ```

3. `number`: This type represents numerical values. Historically in Lua (up to 5.2), all numbers were double-precision floating-point numbers (like `3.14` or `10.0`). Starting with Lua 5.3, numbers can be *either* 64-bit integers (whole numbers like `10`, `-5`, `0`) or double-precision floating-point numbers (`3.14159`). Lua handles the conversion between them automatically in most cases. You generally don't need to worry about the distinction unless doing very specific low-level operations.

```lua
local age = 30          -- Integer
local pi = 3.14159      -- Floating-point
local temperature = -5  -- Integer
```

4. `string`: This type represents sequences of characters – text. You define strings by enclosing text in either single quotes (`'`) or double quotes (`"`). Both work identically, allowing you to easily include one type of quote within a string defined by the other.

```lua
local greeting = "Hello, Lua!"
local question = 'What is your name?'
local quote = "He said, 'Lua is simple!'"
```

You can also create multi-line strings using double square brackets (`[[` and `]]`). Everything between them, including newlines, becomes part of the string.

```lua
local multiLineStory = [[
Once upon a time,
in a land of code,
there was Lua.
]]
```

Strings in Lua are **immutable**, meaning you cannot change a character within an existing string. Operations that seem to modify a string (like concatenation, Chapter 3) actually create a *new* string.

5. `table`: This is Lua's most versatile and powerful data type. Tables are the *only* built-in data structure in Lua. They can be used to represent arrays (lists), dictionaries (maps or associative arrays), objects, and more. A table is essentially a collection of key-value pairs. We'll dedicate **Chapter 6** entirely to tables because they are so fundamental. For now, just recognize { } as creating an empty table.

```
local myArray = { 10, 20, 30 } -- A list-like table
local myRecord = { name = "Bob", age = 42 } -- A dictionary-like table
local emptyTable = {}
```

6. `function`: Functions are blocks of code that perform a specific task. In Lua, functions are "first-class values," meaning they can be stored in variables, passed as arguments to other functions, and returned as results, just like numbers or strings. We'll cover functions in detail in **Chapter 5**.

```
local function sayHello()
  print("Hello!")
end

local greet = sayHello -- Assign function to another variable
greet() -- Call the function using the new variable
```

7. `userdata`: This type allows arbitrary C data to be stored in Lua variables. You use userdata to represent data created by C code (using the C API, see Chapter 14) within your Lua script, often giving it Lua-like behavior using metatables (Chapter 7). You typically encounter this when using libraries written in C or when embedding Lua.

8. `thread`: This type represents an independent thread of execution and is used for **coroutines** (Chapter 11). Coroutines allow for cooperative multitasking, letting you pause and resume functions. Don't confuse this with operating system threads; Lua coroutines run cooperatively within a single OS thread.

## Checking Types with `type()`

Sometimes, you need to know what type of value a variable currently holds. Lua provides the built-in `type()` function for this. It takes one argument (the value or variable you want to check) and returns a string representing its type.

```
local data = "Some text"
print(type(data)) -- Output: string

data = 123
print(type(data)) -- Output: number

data = true
print(type(data)) -- Output: boolean
```

```
data = {}
print(type(data)) -- Output: table

data = nil
print(type(data)) -- Output: nil

data = print -- The print function itself is a value of type 'function'
print(type(data)) -- Output: function
```

# Saying Hello

We've already used it a few times, but let's officially look at `print`. It's a built-in function designed to display values on the console or standard output, primarily for debugging or simple output.

- You can pass one or more arguments to `print`, separated by commas.
- `print` will convert each argument to its string representation.
- It usually inserts a tab character between multiple arguments.
- It automatically adds a newline character at the end, moving the cursor to the next line for subsequent output.

```
local name = "Zara"
local level = 5

print("Welcome!")              -- Output: Welcome!
print(name, level)             -- Output: Zara     5 (with a tab between)
print("Player:", name, "Level:", level)
-- Output: Player: Zara     Level: 5 (tabs between arguments)
```

`print` is your basic window into what your script is doing.

# Your First Program

Let's combine what we've learned into a slightly more structured script than the one in Chapter 1.

Create a file named `user_info.lua` and type the following:

```
-- user_info.lua
-- A simple script to store and display user information
```

```lua
local username = "CodeExplorer"
local age = 28
local hasSubscription = true
local loginCount = 15

print("--- User Profile ---")
print("Username:", username)
print("Age:", age)
print("Active Subscription:", hasSubscription)
print("Total Logins:", loginCount)

-- Let's change some data
age = age + 1 -- Happy Birthday!
loginCount = loginCount + 1

print("--- Updated Info ---")
print("New Age:", age)
print("Login Count Now:", loginCount)
print("Variable 'username' is of type:", type(username))
```

Save the file and run it from your terminal:

```
lua user_info.lua
```

You should see output similar to this (tabs might render as varying spaces):

```
--- User Profile ---
Username:        CodeExplorer
Age:     28
Active Subscription:     true
Total Logins:    15
--- Updated Info ---
New Age:         29
Login Count Now:         16
Variable 'username' is of type:         string
```

This simple script demonstrates:

- Using comments for explanation.
- Declaring local variables to store different data types (string, number, boolean).
- Using the assignment operator (=).
- Using print to display text and variable values.
- Updating variable values.

- Using `type()` to check a variable's data type.

# Chapter Summary

In this chapter, you learned the fundamental grammar of Lua: how statements are structured, the importance of case sensitivity, and how to use comments. You were introduced to variables as named containers for data, emphasizing the use of the `local` keyword. We surveyed Lua's eight data types (`nil`, `boolean`, `number`, `string`, `table`, `function`, `userdata`, `thread`), focusing on the common ones and noting which will be explored further in later chapters. Finally, you practiced using `print` to display information and combined these concepts into a simple program.

Now that you know how to store data, the next step is to learn how to manipulate it. In Chapter 3, we'll dive into expressions and operators – the tools Lua gives you to perform calculations, make comparisons, and combine values.

# 3

# Calculations and Comparisons

In the last chapter, we learned how to store different kinds of information in variables. That's a great start, but programs rarely just store data; they need to *process* it. They perform calculations, compare values, and make decisions based on those comparisons. To do this, Lua uses **expressions** and **operators**. Think of operators as the action verbs of your code – they *do* things with your data. Expressions are like phrases or clauses where you combine data and operators to produce a result. This chapter introduces the essential operators you'll use constantly in your Lua programming journey.

## What Are Expressions?

At its core, an **expression** is anything in your code that Lua can evaluate to produce a value. It could be something very simple:

- A literal value: `10`, `"Hello"`, `true`
- A variable name: `currentScore`, `playerName` (which evaluates to the value stored in the variable)

More interestingly, expressions often involve **operators** – special symbols that perform operations on one or more values (called **operands**).

```
local score = 100
local bonus = 50

local totalScore = score + bonus -- 'score + bonus' is an expression
local isHighScore = totalScore > 1000 -- 'totalScore > 1000' is an expression
local message = "Score: " .. totalScore -- '"Score: " .. totalScore' is an
expression
```

When Lua encounters an expression, it calculates the result. In the examples above:

- `score + bonus` evaluates to `150`.
- `totalScore > 1000` evaluates to `false` (assuming `totalScore` is 150).
- `"Score: " .. totalScore` evaluates to the string `"Score: 150"`.

Understanding how to build and evaluate expressions is fundamental to programming.

# Doing Math

Let's start with the operators you probably recognize from math class. Lua provides standard arithmetic operators to work with `number` values.

| Operator | Name | Example | Result | Description |
|:---:|:---:|:---:|:---:|:---|
| + | Addition | 5 + 3 | 8 | Adds two numbers |
| - | Subtraction | 5 - 3 | 2 | Subtracts the second number from the first |
| * | Multiplication | 5 * 3 | 15 | Multiplies two numbers |
| / | Division | 5 / 2 | 2.5 | Divides the first number by the second (always results in a float since Lua 5.3) |
| ^ | Exponentiation | 5 ^ 2 | 25 | Raises the first number to the power of the second |
| % | Modulo | 5 % 2 | 1 | Returns the remainder of a division |
| - | Unary Minus | -5 | -5 | Negates a number |

```
local width = 10
local height = 5
local area = width * height -- area will be 50

local radius = 3
local circleArea = math.pi * (radius ^ 2) -- using pi from the math library
-- circleArea will be approximately 28.27

local items = 17
local groupSize = 5
local leftover = items % groupSize -- leftover will be 2
```

# Order of Operations

What happens when you combine multiple operators in one expression, like 3 + 5 *
2? Does Lua add first (3+5=8, 8*2=16) or multiply first (5*2=10, 3+10=13)?

Like standard mathematics, Lua follows an **order of operations** (often remembered
by acronyms like PEMDAS/BODMAS). Operators have different **precedence** levels:

1. ^ (Exponentiation) - Highest precedence
2. Unary - (Negation)
3. *, /, % (Multiplication, Division, Modulo)
4. +, - (Addition, Subtraction) - Lowest precedence

Operators with the same precedence are usually evaluated from left to right (except
for ^, which is right-associative: 2^3^2 is 2^(3^2) = 2^9 = 512).

So, in 3 + 5 * 2, multiplication (*) has higher precedence than addition (+), so 5 * 2
is calculated first (10), and then 3 + 10 is calculated, resulting in 13.

When in doubt, or to override the default order, use **parentheses** (). Expressions
inside parentheses are always evaluated first.

```
local result1 = 3 + 5 * 2   -- result1 is 13 (multiplication first)
local result2 = (3 + 5) * 2 -- result2 is 16 (addition first due to parentheses)
```

Using parentheses even when not strictly necessary can often make your code much
clearer and easier to understand.

# Checking Relationships

Often, you need to compare values. Are two values equal? Is one greater than the other? **Relational operators** perform these comparisons and always produce a `boolean` result (`true` or `false`).

| Operator | Name | Example | Result | Description |
|----------|------|---------|--------|-------------|
| == | Equality | 5 == 5 | 1 | Returns `true` if operands are equal |
| ~= | Inequality (Not Equal) | 5 ~= 3 | 1 | Returns `true` if operands are not equal |
| < | Less Than | 5 < 3 | 0 | Returns `true` if left operand is less than right |
| > | Greater Than | 5 > 3 | 1 | Returns `true` if left operand is greater than right |
| <= | Less Than or Equal To | 5 <= 5 | 1 | Returns `true` if left is less than or equal to right |
| >= | Greater Than or Equal To | 5 >= 3 | 1 | Returns `true` if left is greater than or equal to right |

**Crucial Pitfall:** Remember that == (double equals) is for **comparison**, while = (single equals) is for **assignment**. Mixing these up is a very common beginner mistake!

```
local myScore = 1500
local highScore = 2000
local attempts = 3
local maxAttempts = 5

print(myScore == highScore)    -- Output: false
print(myScore ~= highScore)    -- Output: true
print(myScore > highScore)     -- Output: false
print(attempts < maxAttempts)  -- Output: true
print(attempts >= 3)           -- Output: true
```

You can compare numbers and strings. String comparison is done lexicographically (like in a dictionary, based on character codes).

```
print("apple" < "banana") -- Output: true
print("Zebra" > "apple")  -- Output: false (uppercase Z comes before lowercase
a)
print("hello" == "hello") -- Output: true
print("Hello" == "hello") -- Output: false (case-sensitive)
```

Comparing values of *different* types using relational operators (other than ~=) generally results in `false`. Equality (==) only returns `true` if both the values and the types are the same. Inequality (~=) returns `true` if the types are different or if the values are different within the same type.

```
print(10 == "10") -- Output: false (number vs string)
print(10 ~= "10") -- Output: true
```

# Making Logical Choices

Sometimes you need to combine multiple conditions. Is the score high *and* are there attempts left? Is the game over *or* did the player quit? **Logical operators** work with boolean values (or values interpreted as boolean) to produce a boolean result.

Lua has three logical operators: and, or, and not.

## and

The and operator returns `true` only if **both** its left and right operands are considered true. If the left operand is false (or `nil`), and doesn't even evaluate the right operand (this is called **short-circuit evaluation**) because the result must be false anyway.

A special characteristic of Lua's and is that it returns the *first* operand if it's false (`false` or `nil`), otherwise it returns the *second* operand.

```
local hasFuel = true
local hasEngine = true
print(hasFuel and hasEngine) -- Output: true (returns second operand)

local hasKey = false
local isDoorLocked = true
print(hasKey and isDoorLocked) -- Output: false (returns first operand, hasKey)
```

```
local score = 100
local lives = 0
print(lives > 0 and score > 1000) -- Output: false (lives > 0 is false, returns
it)
                                  -- 'score > 1000' is never evaluated
```

## or

The or operator returns true if **at least one** of its operands is considered true. If the left operand is true, or short-circuits and doesn't evaluate the right operand, because the result must be true.

Lua's or returns the *first* operand if it is considered true, otherwise it returns the *second* operand. This is often used to provide default values:

```
local isPaused = false
local isGameOver = true
print(isPaused or isGameOver) -- Output: true (isGameOver is true, returned)

local hasPowerUp = true
local isInvincible = false
print(hasPowerUp or isInvincible) -- Output: true (hasPowerUp is true, returned)

-- Common pattern for default values:
local playerName = requestedName or "Guest"
-- If requestedName is nil or false, playerName becomes "Guest".
-- Otherwise, playerName becomes the value of requestedName.
print(playerName)
```

## not

The not operator is unary (it takes only one operand) and simply inverts the boolean value. If the operand is true, not returns false. If the operand is false (or nil), not returns true.

```
local isEnabled = true
print(not isEnabled) -- Output: false

local isEmpty = false
print(not isEmpty) -- Output: true

print(not nil) -- Output: true
```

```
print(not 0)    -- Output: false (see truthiness below)
```

## Truthiness in Lua

This is a key concept! When Lua expects a boolean value (in `if` statements, `while` loops, or as operands to logical operators), how does it treat values of other types?

The rule is simple: **In Lua, only `false` and `nil` are considered false.** Everything else – numbers (including `0`), strings (including the empty string `""`), tables, functions – is considered **true** in a boolean context. This is different from some other languages where `0` or `""` might be treated as false.

```
if 0 then
  print("Zero is considered true in Lua!") -- This will be printed
end

if "" then
  print("Empty string is considered true in Lua!") -- This will be printed
end

if {} then
  print("An empty table is considered true in Lua!") -- This will be printed
end

if not nil then
  print("Not nil is true") -- This will be printed
end

if not false then
  print("Not false is true") -- This will be printed
end
```

Understanding truthiness is vital for correctly using logical operators and control structures (Chapter 4).

# Working with Text

How do you join strings together? Lua uses the **concatenation** operator, which is represented by two dots (`..`).

```
local firstName = "Ada"
local lastName = "Lovelace"
```

```
local fullName = firstName .. " " .. lastName -- Note the space added

print(fullName) -- Output: Ada Lovelace

local item = "potion"
local quantity = 3
local message = "You found " .. quantity .. " " .. item .. "s!"

print(message) -- Output: You found 3 potions!
```

Lua automatically converts numbers to strings when you try to concatenate them with a string, which is quite convenient.

# Measuring Length

Sometimes you need to know how long a string is (how many characters it contains) or, as we'll see in Chapter 6, how many elements are in the sequential part of a table. Lua provides the unary **length operator**, denoted by a hash symbol (#).

```
local greeting = "Hello"
print(#greeting) -- Output: 5

local emptyString = ""
print(#emptyString) -- Output: 0

local sentence = "Lua is fun!"
local len = #sentence
print("The sentence has " .. len .. " characters.")
-- Output: The sentence has 11 characters.
```

*Important Note:* For strings, # returns the number of **bytes**, not necessarily the number of characters, especially when dealing with multi-byte character encodings like UTF-8. For standard ASCII text, bytes and characters are the same. Lua 5.3+ introduced the utf8 library (Chapter 12) for correctly handling UTF-8 character counts.

The length operator also works on tables used as arrays (with sequential integer keys starting from 1), but we'll explore that in detail in Chapter 6. #{} evaluates to 0.

# Operator Precedence Revisited

We discussed precedence for arithmetic operators, but how do all the operators we've learned relate to each other? Here's a simplified overview from highest precedence to lowest:

1. `^` (Exponentiation)
2. `not`, `#`, `-` (Unary operators: logical not, length, negation)
3. `*`, `/`, `%` (Multiplication, division, modulo)
4. `+`, `-` (Addition, subtraction)
5. `..` (Concatenation)
6. `<`, `>`, `<=`, `>=`, `~=`, `==` (Relational operators)
7. `and` (Logical and)
8. `or` (Logical or) - Lowest precedence

**Example:** `1 + 2 < 5 and #("hi") == 2`

1. Unary #: `#("hi")` becomes 2. Expression: `1 + 2 < 5 and 2 == 2`
2. Addition +: `1 + 2` becomes 3. Expression: `3 < 5 and 2 == 2`
3. Relational < and == (evaluated left-to-right at same level):
   - `3 < 5` becomes true. Expression: `true and 2 == 2`
   - `2 == 2` becomes true. Expression: `true and true`
4. Logical and: `true and true` becomes true. Final result: `true`.

While knowing the precedence rules is helpful, **using parentheses () is often the best way to ensure correctness and improve readability.** Don't make others (or your future self) guess the evaluation order!

```
-- Less clear:
local result = a + b * c ^ d > limit or not finished

-- Much clearer:
local power = c ^ d
local product = b * power
local sum = a + product
local comparison = sum > limit
local finalResult = comparison or (not finished)
```

Even if you don't break it down quite that much, parentheses help:

```
local result = ((a + (b * (c ^ d))) > limit) or (not finished)
```

# Chapter Summary

In this chapter, you learned how to manipulate data using Lua's operators. We covered arithmetic operators (+, -, *, /, ^, %) for calculations, relational operators (==, ~=, <, >, <=, >=) for comparisons, and logical operators (and, or, not) for combining boolean conditions. You also learned how to join strings using the concatenation operator (..) and find the length of strings (and soon, tables) with the length operator (#). We discussed operator precedence and the importance of parentheses for clarity, along with the crucial concept of **truthiness** in Lua (only `nil` and `false` are false).

These expressions that produce `true` or `false` results are the foundation for controlling the flow of your programs. Now that you can evaluate conditions, the next chapter will show you how to use `if` statements to make decisions and loops to repeat actions based on these conditions.

# 4

# Making Decisions and Repeating Tasks

So far, the Lua scripts we've written have been like following a straight road – they execute one instruction after another, from top to bottom, without deviation. But real-world tasks often involve choices and repetition. Think about giving directions: " *If* the traffic light is red, stop; *otherwise*, go." Or instructions for baking: "*Repeat* kneading the dough *until* it's smooth." Programming needs similar capabilities. In Chapter 3, you learned how to create expressions that evaluate to true or false. Now, we'll use those conditions to build programs that can make decisions using if **statements** and repeat actions using **loops** (while, repeat, and for). These **control flow structures** are what make programs dynamic and intelligent.

## Choosing Paths

Imagine you're walking down a path, and you reach a fork. You need to decide which way to go based on some condition (maybe a signpost). The if statement is Lua's way of handling these forks in the road.

# The Basic if Statement

The simplest if statement executes a block of code *only if* a specific condition is true (remembering Lua's truthiness rules from Chapter 3: anything other than `false` or `nil` is considered true).

The structure looks like this:

```
if condition then
  -- Code to execute if the condition is true
  -- This is often called the 'then' block
end
```

- `if`: The keyword that starts the conditional block.
- `condition`: An expression that evaluates to a boolean (`true`/`false`) or a value treated as such.
- `then`: The keyword that marks the beginning of the code block to execute if the condition is true.
- `end`: The keyword that marks the end of the `if` statement block. **Every `if` needs a corresponding `end`!**

Let's see it in action:

```
local temperature = 30

if temperature > 25 then
  print("It's a warm day!")
  print("Don't forget sunscreen.")
end

print("Weather check complete.") -- This line runs regardless
```

**Output:**

```
It's a warm day!
Don't forget sunscreen.
Weather check complete.
```

If we change `temperature` to 15, the condition `temperature > 25` becomes `false`, and the code inside the then...end block is skipped entirely.

**Output (if temperature = 15):**

```
Weather check complete.
```

## Adding Alternatives with `else`

What if you want to do something different when the condition is *false*? Like saying, "If it's raining, take an umbrella; otherwise, wear sunglasses." Lua provides the `else` keyword for this.

```
if condition then
  -- Code to execute if the condition is true
else
  -- Code to execute if the condition is false
end
```

Example:

```
local accountBalance = 45.50
local itemCost = 60.00

if accountBalance >= itemCost then
  print("Purchase successful!")
  accountBalance = accountBalance - itemCost
else
  print("Insufficient funds.")
  print("Please add money to your account.")
end

print("Final balance:", accountBalance)
```

**Output:**

```
Insufficient funds.
Please add money to your account.
Final balance: 45.5
```

If `accountBalance` was `100.00`, the `then` block would execute instead.

## Handling Multiple Choices with `elseif`

Sometimes you have more than two possibilities. Imagine sorting mail: *if* it's a bill, put it in the red folder; *else if* it's a letter, put it in the blue folder; *else if* it's junk mail, put it in the bin; *otherwise* (if it's none of those), put it on the desk. Lua uses elseif (note: one word!) for these chained conditions.

```lua
if condition1 then
  -- Code for condition1 being true
elseif condition2 then
  -- Code for condition1 false, but condition2 true
elseif condition3 then
  -- Code for 1 and 2 false, but condition3 true
else
  -- Code if NONE of the above conditions are true
end
```

Lua checks the conditions in order. As soon as it finds a true condition, it executes the corresponding block and then skips the rest of the elseif/else chain, jumping straight to the final end. The final else is optional; if omitted, nothing happens if none of the if/elseif conditions are true.

```lua
local score = 78

if score >= 90 then
  print("Grade: A")
elseif score >= 80 then
  print("Grade: B")
elseif score >= 70 then
  print("Grade: C")
elseif score >= 60 then
  print("Grade: D")
else
  print("Grade: F")
end

print("Grading complete.")
```

**Output:**

```
Grade: C
Grading complete.
```

Because score >= 90 is false, and score >= 80 is false, but score >= 70 is true, it prints "Grade: C" and skips the remaining elseif and else.

## Nesting `if` Statements

You can put `if` statements inside other `if` statements. This is called **nesting**.

```
local isLoggedIn = true
local userRole = "admin"

if isLoggedIn then
  print("Welcome back!")
  if userRole == "admin" then
    print("Admin panel access granted.")
  elseif userRole == "editor" then
    print("You can edit content.")
  else
    print("Standard user access.")
  end
else
  print("Please log in to continue.")
end
```

**Output:**

```
Welcome back!
Admin panel access granted.
```

While nesting is powerful, be careful! Too many levels of nested `if` statements can make code very difficult to read and understand. Sometimes, restructuring your code or using functions (Chapter 5) can help simplify complex nested logic.

# Repeating Yourself

Often, you need to perform the same (or a similar) action multiple times. Imagine counting from 1 to 10, processing every item in a list, or waiting for user input. Instead of writing the same code lines over and over, you use **loops**. Loops execute a block of code repeatedly as long as (or until) a certain condition is met.

## The `while` Loop

The `while` loop is perhaps the most fundamental loop type. It repeats a block of code **as long as** a specified condition remains true. The condition is checked *before* each potential execution of the loop body.

The structure is:

```
while condition do
  -- Code to repeat (loop body)
  -- IMPORTANT: Something inside the loop should eventually
  -- make the condition false!
end
```

- while: Keyword starting the loop.
- condition: The boolean expression checked before each iteration.
- do: Keyword marking the start of the loop body.
- end: Keyword marking the end of the loop body.

Example: Countdown

```
local countdown = 5

print("Starting countdown...")
while countdown > 0 do
  print(countdown .. "...")
  countdown = countdown - 1 -- Crucial step! Changes the condition variable
end

print("Blast off!")
```

**Output:**

```
Starting countdown...
5...
4...
3...
2...
1...
Blast off!
```

**Crucial Pitfall: Infinite Loops!** What happens if the condition in a while loop *never* becomes false? The loop will run forever (or until you manually stop the program). This is called an **infinite loop** and is a common bug.

```
local counter = 0
while counter < 5 do
  print("This might run forever!")
  -- OOPS! We forgot to increment counter. It will always be 0.
```

```
   -- counter = counter + 1 -- This line is missing!
end
-- This program will never reach here unless you stop it.
```

Always ensure that something inside your `while` loop body will eventually cause the condition to evaluate to `false` or `nil`.

# The `repeat...until` Loop

The `repeat...until` loop is similar to `while`, but with two key differences:

1. The condition is checked *after* the loop body executes.
2. The loop continues *until* the condition becomes true (the opposite logic of `while`).

This means the loop body is **always executed at least once**.

The structure is:

```
repeat
  -- Code to repeat (loop body)
  -- Again, something should eventually make the condition true.
until condition
```

- repeat: Keyword starting the loop.
- until: Keyword marking the end of the loop body and specifying the exit condition.
- condition: The boolean expression checked *after* each iteration. The loop stops when this is `true`.

Example: Simple menu prompt

```
local choice

repeat
  print("\n--- MENU ---")
  print("1. Start Game")
  print("2. Load Game")
  print("3. Quit")
  print("Enter your choice:")
  -- In a real program, you'd use io.read() here to get input
  -- For this example, let's simulate input:
  choice = 3 -- Simulating the user choosing 'Quit'
```

```
    print("User chose: " .. choice) -- Show simulated choice

    if choice < 1 or choice > 3 then
      print("Invalid choice, please try again.")
    end

until choice >= 1 and choice <= 3 -- Loop until choice is valid (1, 2, or 3)

print("Processing choice: " .. choice)
```

**Output:**

```
--- MENU ---
1. Start Game
2. Load Game
3. Quit
Enter your choice:
User chose: 3
Processing choice: 3
```

Because the condition choice >= 1 and choice <= 3 is checked *after* the print statements and the simulated input, the menu is always displayed at least once. If the user entered an invalid choice (e.g., 5), the condition would be false, and the loop would repeat.

# The Numeric for Loop

When you know exactly how many times you want to repeat something, or you want to iterate through a sequence of numbers, the numeric for loop is often the cleanest solution.

The structure is:

```
for variable = startValue, endValue, stepValue do
  -- Loop body
end
```

- for: Keyword starting the loop.
- variable: A **new local variable** created just for this loop. It holds the current value in the sequence during each iteration. You don't need to declare it with local beforehand; the for loop does this automatically.

- startValue: The initial value assigned to `variable`.
- endValue: The loop continues as long as `variable` hasn't passed this value (considering the step).
- stepValue (Optional): The amount to add to `variable` after each iteration. If omitted, the default step is 1. It can be negative for counting down.
- do/end: Mark the loop body.

Example: Counting up

```
print("Counting up:")
for i = 1, 5 do -- Step defaults to 1
  print("i =", i)
end
```

**Output:**

```
Counting up:
i = 1
i = 2
i = 3
i = 4
i = 5
```

Example: Counting down with a step

```
print("Counting down by 2s:")
for count = 10, 0, -2 do -- Explicit negative step
  print("Count:", count)
end
```

**Output:**

```
Counting down by 2s:
Count: 10
Count: 8
Count: 6
Count: 4
Count: 2
Count: 0
```

**Important Notes:**

- The control variable (i or count in the examples) is **local** to the loop body. You cannot access its final value after the loop finishes.
- The startValue, endValue, and stepValue are evaluated **only once** before the loop starts. Changing the variables used to set these values *inside* the loop will not affect the number of iterations.

## The Generic for Loop (A Sneak Peek)

Lua has another, even more powerful type of for loop called the **generic for**. This loop is designed to iterate over the elements of a collection, most commonly a **table** (which we'll dive into in **Chapter 6**).

While we won't go into the full details yet, you'll often see it used with **iterator functions** like pairs and ipairs to walk through the contents of a table.

A quick glimpse (don't worry about fully understanding this yet):

```lua
local colors = { "red", "green", "blue" }

print("Colors in the list:")
-- ipairs iterates over the integer keys (1, 2, 3...)
for index, value in ipairs(colors) do
  print("Index:", index, "Value:", value)
end

local config = { width = 800, height = 600, title = "My App" }

print("\nConfiguration settings:")
-- pairs iterates over all key-value pairs (order not guaranteed)
for key, val in pairs(config) do
  print("Key:", key, "Value:", val)
end
```

**Output:**

```
Colors in the list:
Index: 1        Value: red
Index: 2        Value: green
Index: 3        Value: blue

Configuration settings:
Key: width      Value: 800
Key: title      Value: My App
Key: height     Value: 600
```

*(Note: The order from* pairs *might vary)*

The generic for loop is incredibly useful for working with tables, Lua's primary data structure. We'll explore it properly when we learn about tables in Chapter 6.

# Changing the Flow

Sometimes, you need to exit a loop earlier than its normal condition would allow. Maybe you found the specific item you were searching for, or an error occurred.

## Exiting Early

The break statement immediately terminates the innermost while, repeat, or for loop it is currently inside. Execution continues with the statement immediately following the ended loop.

```lua
local items = { "apple", "banana", "STOP", "orange", "grape" }

print("Processing items until STOP is found:")
for index, item in ipairs(items) do
  if item == "STOP" then
    print("Found STOP signal at index", index)
    break -- Exit the 'for' loop immediately
  end
  print("Processing item:", item)
  -- Some processing would happen here
end

print("Loop finished or broken.")
```

**Output:**

```
Processing items until STOP is found:
Processing item: apple
Processing item: banana
Found STOP signal at index 3
Loop finished or broken.
```

Notice that "orange" and "grape" were never processed because break exited the loop when "STOP" was encountered.

# Advanced Control

Lua includes a goto statement, common in older languages but often discouraged in modern programming. It allows you to jump unconditionally to another point in your code marked by a **label**.

## What Are Labels?

A label is simply a name enclosed in double colons ::.

```
::myLabel::
-- Some code here
```

## Using goto

The goto statement then jumps execution directly to the specified label.

```
local count = 0
::loopStart:: -- Define a label
count = count + 1
print("Count:", count)
if count < 3 then
  goto loopStart -- Jump back to the label
end
print("Loop finished using goto.")
```

**Output:**

```
Count: 1
Count: 2
Count: 3
Loop finished using goto.
```

## Why goto Can Be Confusing

While the example above works, goto can make code extremely difficult to follow, especially in larger programs. Jumping around arbitrarily breaks the normal flow of execution and can lead to what's called "spaghetti code" – tangled, hard-to-debug logic.

**Generally, you should avoid** goto. Most tasks that might seem to require goto can be accomplished more clearly using standard loops (while, repeat, for), if statements, break, and well-structured functions (Chapter 5).

There are very rare, specific situations where goto might be considered the least awkward solution (like breaking out of deeply nested loops, which break cannot do directly, or implementing complex finite state machines), but these are advanced cases. As a beginner, focus on mastering the standard control flow structures first. If you find yourself reaching for goto, step back and see if there's a cleaner way using if, loops, or functions.

# Chapter Summary

In this chapter, you've gained control over the execution path of your Lua programs. You learned to make decisions using if, elseif, and else statements, allowing your code to react differently based on conditions established in Chapter 3. You also mastered repetition using loops: the condition-first while loop, the run-at-least-once repeat...until loop, and the counter-based numeric for loop. We had a sneak peek at the powerful generic for loop (more in Chapter 6!) for iterating over collections. We saw how break lets you exit loops early and discussed the goto statement with a strong recommendation to use it only with extreme caution, if at all.

These control structures are the fundamental tools for creating logic. You can now write programs that do more than just execute commands in sequence. Often, the code you place inside these if blocks and loops performs a specific, reusable task. In the next chapter, we'll learn how to package these reusable blocks of code into **functions**, making our programs more organized, efficient, and easier to manage.

# 5

# Functions

In the previous chapter, we learned how to control the flow of our programs using `if` statements and loops. As your programs grow, you'll often find yourself needing to perform the same sequence of actions in multiple places. Copying and pasting code works, but it's inefficient and error-prone. If you find a bug or need to make a change, you have to update it everywhere you pasted it! Wouldn't it be better to write that code *once* and just call it whenever you need it? That's precisely what **functions** allow you to do. Functions are named blocks of code designed to perform a specific task. They are the fundamental building blocks for organizing larger Lua programs, making your code cleaner, easier to reuse, and much simpler to understand and maintain.

## What Are Functions?

Think of a function like a recipe. A recipe has a name (e.g., "Bake Chocolate Cake"), a set of ingredients it needs (parameters), and a series of steps to follow (the function body). When you want a chocolate cake, you "call" the recipe, provide the ingredients (arguments), and follow the steps to get a result (the cake, or a return value).

In Lua, a function is a block of code that you can:

- **Give a name to:** So you can easily refer to it.
- **Call (or invoke):** To execute the code inside it.
- **Pass data into:** Using **parameters**.
- **Get data out of:** Using **return values**.

Why bother wrapping code in functions?

- **Organization:** Functions break down complex problems into smaller, manageable pieces. Each function handles one specific part of the task.
- **Reusability:** Write the code once, call it many times from different parts of your program. This saves time and reduces errors.
- **Abstraction:** When you call a function, you often don't need to know *how* it performs its task internally, only *what* it does. This hides complexity and makes your main code easier to read. For example, you call `print()` without needing to know the complex details of how it interacts with the operating system to display text on the screen.

# Defining Your Own Functions

You create a function in Lua using the `function` keyword. The most common way looks like this:

```
function functionName(parameter1, parameter2, ...) -- Parameters are optional
    -- Code block (the function body)
    -- This code runs when the function is called.
    -- It can use the parameters passed to it.
    -- It might return a value using the 'return' keyword.
end
```

Let's break it down:

- `function`: The keyword that signals the start of a function definition.
- `functionName`: The name you choose for your function. It follows the same naming rules as variables (letters, numbers, underscores, cannot start with a number, case-sensitive). Choose descriptive names!
- `(parameter1, parameter2, ...)`: An optional list of **parameter** names, separated by commas, enclosed in parentheses. Parameters act like local variables within the function, receiving the values passed in when the function is called. If the function doesn't need any input, you just use empty parentheses `()`.
- `-- Code block`: The sequence of Lua statements that make up the function's task. This is the **function body**.
- `end`: The keyword that marks the end of the function definition.

Here's a simple function definition:

```
-- Defines a function named 'greet' that takes one parameter 'name'
```

```
function greet(name)
  local message = "Hello there, " .. name .. "!"
  print(message)
end
```

This code *defines* the function `greet`, but it doesn't run the code inside it yet. It's like writing down the recipe but not actually baking the cake.

# Calling Functions

To execute the code inside a function, you **call** it by using its name followed by parentheses (). If the function expects arguments (values for its parameters), you put them inside the parentheses.

```
-- Call the greet function, passing the string "Alice" as the argument
greet("Alice")

-- Call it again with a different argument
greet("Bob")
```

**Output:**

```
Hello there, Alice!
Hello there, Bob!
```

When `greet("Alice")` is called:

1. The value `"Alice"` (the **argument**) is assigned to the `name` **parameter** inside the greet function.
2. The code inside `greet` executes. The local variable `message` becomes `"Hello there, Alice!"`.
3. `print(message)` displays the greeting.

# Passing Information

Parameters and arguments are two sides of the same coin, relating to how functions receive input.

- **Parameters:** These are the variable names listed inside the parentheses in the *function definition*. They act as placeholders for the values that will be supplied when the function is called. They are always local to the function.
- **Arguments:** These are the actual values you pass *to* the function when you *call* it.

```lua
-- Definition: 'width' and 'height' are PARAMETERS
function calculateArea(width, height)
  local area = width * height
  print("The area is:", area)
end

-- Call: 10 and 5 are ARGUMENTS
calculateArea(10, 5)
```

**Output:**

```
The area is: 50
```

Lua matches arguments to parameters based on their **position**. The first argument goes to the first parameter, the second argument to the second parameter, and so on.

- If you provide *fewer* arguments than parameters, the extra parameters receive the value nil.
- If you provide *more* arguments than parameters, the extra arguments are simply ignored (unless the function is designed to handle variable arguments, see below).

```lua
function displayInfo(name, age, city)
  print("Name:", name, "Age:", age, "City:", city)
end

displayInfo("Carlos", 30, "Cairo", "Extra Argument") -- "Extra Argument" ignored
displayInfo("Diana", 25) -- city parameter becomes nil
```

**Output:**

```
Name:    Carlos  Age:    30    City:    Cairo
Name:    Diana   Age:    25    City:    nil
```

# Getting Results

Many functions compute a result that the calling code needs to use. Printing inside the function is useful for display, but often you want the function to *give back* a value. This is done using the `return` keyword.

When Lua encounters `return`, it immediately exits the function and sends the specified value(s) back to the place where the function was called.

```lua
function addNumbers(num1, num2)
  local sum = num1 + num2
  return sum -- Send the calculated sum back
  -- Code after 'return' in the same block will NOT be executed
  print("This line is never reached.")
end

-- Call the function and store the returned value in a variable
local result = addNumbers(5, 3)
print("The result of addition is:", result)

-- You can also use the returned value directly in an expression
local anotherResult = addNumbers(10, 20) * 2
print("Another calculation:", anotherResult)
```

**Output:**

```
The result of addition is: 8
Another calculation: 60
```

A function can return without any value (`return` on its own), which is equivalent to returning `nil`. If a function reaches its end without encountering a `return` statement, it also implicitly returns `nil`.

## Lua's Special Power

One of Lua's distinctive features is that functions can easily return **multiple values**. Simply list the values after the `return` keyword, separated by commas.

```lua
function getCoordinates()
  local x = 100
  local y = 250
  return x, y -- Return two values
```

```
end

-- Assign the returned values to multiple variables
local posX, posY = getCoordinates()
print("Position X:", posX)
print("Position Y:", posY)

-- If you provide fewer variables, extra return values are discarded
local firstValue = getCoordinates()
print("Only got first value:", firstValue)

-- If you provide more variables, extra variables get nil
local val1, val2, val3 = getCoordinates()
print("Values:", val1, val2, val3)
```

**Output:**

```
Position X:      100
Position Y:      250
Only got first value:    100
Values: 100     250     nil
```

This ability to return multiple values is very convenient and often avoids the need to wrap results in a table just to return them.

# Flexible Functions

What if you want to create a function that can accept *any* number of arguments? Like the print function, which can take one, two, or many arguments. Lua provides the **varargs** feature using three dots (. . .) as the last parameter in the function definition.

```
function sumAll(...)
  local total = 0
  -- The '...' represents a list of arguments passed
  -- We can capture them into a table using { ... }
  local args = { ... } -- Pack arguments into a table named 'args'

  -- Now we can iterate through the table (using generic 'for', Chapter 6)
  for i, value in ipairs(args) do
    total = total + value
  end
  return total
end
```

```
local sum1 = sumAll(1, 2, 3)            -- Pass 3 arguments
local sum2 = sumAll(10, 20, 30, 40, 50) -- Pass 5 arguments
local sum3 = sumAll()                    -- Pass 0 arguments

print("Sum 1:", sum1) -- Output: Sum 1: 6
print("Sum 2:", sum2) -- Output: Sum 2: 150
print("Sum 3:", sum3) -- Output: Sum 3: 0
```

Inside a vararg function, ... behaves somewhat like a list. You can:

- **Pack them into a table**: {...} creates a new table containing all the variable arguments. This is often the easiest way to work with them.
- **Use** select('#', ...): This returns the *number* of variable arguments passed.
- **Use** select(n, ...): This returns the *n*-th variable argument and all subsequent ones.

```
function describe(...)
  local numArgs = select('#', ...)
  print("Number of arguments:", numArgs)

  if numArgs > 0 then
    local firstArg = select(1, ...)
    print("First argument:", firstArg)
  end
  if numArgs > 1 then
    local secondArg = select(2, ...)
    print("Second argument:", secondArg)
  end
end

describe("apple", true, 100)
```

**Output:**

```
Number of arguments: 3
First argument: apple
Second argument: true
```

Variable arguments provide great flexibility for functions that need to handle varying inputs.

# Where Variables Live

Remember the `local` keyword we emphasized in Chapter 2? Its importance becomes even clearer when working with functions. **Scope** refers to the region of your code where a variable is accessible.

- **Global Variables:** If you declare a variable *without* using the `local` keyword (either outside any function or inside one), it becomes a **global** variable. Globals are stored in a special hidden table (called the environment table, often _G) and are accessible from *anywhere* in your entire Lua program (including inside any function).

```lua
appName = "My Awesome App" -- Global variable (no 'local')

function printAppName()
  print("Running:", appName) -- Accessing the global variable
end

printAppName() -- Output: Running: My Awesome App
```

While easy to use, excessive use of global variables is generally **bad practice**. Why?

- **Name Clashes:** Different parts of your code (or different modules you use) might accidentally use the same global variable name, overwriting each other's values and causing hard-to-debug errors.
- **Hidden Dependencies:** It's hard to tell what parts of the code a function relies on if it uses many globals.
- **Garbage Collection:** Global variables are typically never automatically garbage collected (Chapter 13) because the program always maintains a reference to them through the global table.
- **Local Variables:** Variables declared using the `local` keyword have **local scope**. Their visibility is limited to the **block** of code where they are defined.

- A block is typically the code between do and end, then and end, function and end, or simply the entire file (chunk).
- Parameters of a function are also local to that function.

```lua
local globalMessage = "I am global (to this file)"

function myFunction(param) -- 'param' is local to myFunction
  local localVar = "I am local to myFunction"
```

```lua
    print(localVar)
    print(param)
    print(globalMessage) -- Can access locals from containing blocks

    if param > 10 then
      local nestedLocal = "I am local to the 'if' block"
      print(nestedLocal)
    end
    -- print(nestedLocal) -- ERROR! nestedLocal is not visible here
  end

  myFunction(15)
  -- print(localVar) -- ERROR! localVar is not visible here
  -- print(param)    -- ERROR! param is not visible here
  print(globalMessage) -- This works
```

**Always prefer** `local` **variables.** They make your code cleaner, safer, and easier to reason about. Only use globals when you specifically need widely shared state, and even then, consider alternatives like passing values through function arguments or storing them in modules (Chapter 10).

# Functions Are Values Too!

This is a cornerstone concept in Lua: **functions are first-class values** (or first-class citizens). This means you can treat functions just like any other data type (like numbers, strings, or tables):

- **Assign functions to variables:**

```lua
function sayHi()
  print("Hi!")
end

local greetingFunction = sayHi -- Assign the function itself
greetingFunction() -- Call it using the new variable name
-- Output: Hi!
```

This is so common that Lua provides syntactic sugar for it. The standard `function foo() ... end` definition is equivalent to `local foo = function() ... end`. The second form highlights that you're creating an anonymous function and assigning it to a local variable.

- **Store functions in tables:**

```lua
local operations = {}
operations.add = function(a, b) return a + b end
operations.subtract = function(a, b) return a - b end

print(operations.add(10, 5)) -- Output: 15
```

This is fundamental to how object-oriented programming is often done in Lua (Chapter 15).

- **Pass functions as arguments to other functions (Callbacks):**

```lua
function doMath(a, b, mathOperation)
  local result = mathOperation(a, b) -- Call the passed-in function
  print("Result:", result)
end

function multiply(x, y)
  return x * y
end

doMath(7, 6, multiply) -- Pass the 'multiply' function as an argument
-- Output: Result: 42

-- Pass an anonymous function directly:
doMath(7, 6, function(x, y) return x / y end)
-- Output: Result: 1.1666666666667
```

- **Return functions from other functions:**

```lua
function createGreeter(greetingWord)
  -- Return a NEW function
  return function(name)
    print(greetingWord .. ", " .. name .. "!")
  end
end

local sayHello = createGreeter("Hello")
local sayBonjour = createGreeter("Bonjour")

sayHello("World")    -- Output: Hello, World!
sayBonjour("Monde") -- Output: Bonjour, Monde!
```

This last example leads us directly into closures.

The first-class nature of functions makes Lua incredibly flexible and powerful, enabling programming patterns common in functional programming languages.

# Understanding Closures

Closures are a direct consequence of functions being first-class values and Lua using **lexical scoping**.

- **Lexical Scoping:** When a function is defined, it remembers the environment (the set of local variables it can access) from where it was defined, not where it is called.
- **Closure:** A closure is a function combined with the environment it "captured" when it was created. This means a function can still access the local variables of its *enclosing* function, even *after* the enclosing function has finished executing!

Let's revisit the `createGreeter` example:

```lua
function createGreeter(greetingWord) -- Enclosing function
  -- 'greetingWord' is a local variable of createGreeter

  local greeterFunc = function(name) -- Inner function
    -- This inner function can access 'greetingWord' from its
    -- enclosing environment, even after createGreeter returns.
    print(greetingWord .. ", " .. name .. "!")
  end

  return greeterFunc -- Return the inner function
end

local sayHello = createGreeter("Hello") -- greetingWord="Hello" is captured
local sayBonjour = createGreeter("Bonjour") -- greetingWord="Bonjour" is
captured

-- When sayHello is called, it still remembers greetingWord was "Hello"
sayHello("Alice") -- Output: Hello, Alice!

-- When sayBonjour is called, it remembers greetingWord was "Bonjour"
sayBonjour("Bob") -- Output: Bonjour, Bob!
```

Each function returned by `createGreeter` (sayHello, sayBonjour) is a **closure**. They package the function code *and* the specific value of `greetingWord` that existed when they were created.

Closures are powerful for creating private state, building iterators, implementing callbacks with context, and much more.

Here's another classic closure example: a counter factory.

```
function createCounter()
  local count = 0 -- This local variable will be captured
  return function() -- Return the closure
    count = count + 1
    return count
  end
end

local counter1 = createCounter()
local counter2 = createCounter()

print(counter1()) -- Output: 1
print(counter1()) -- Output: 2 (Uses its own 'count')
print(counter2()) -- Output: 1 (Uses its own separate 'count')
print(counter1()) -- Output: 3
```

Each counter function maintains its own independent count variable captured from its specific call to createCounter.

# Functions Calling Themselves

**Recursion** occurs when a function calls itself, either directly or indirectly. It's a way to solve problems by breaking them down into smaller, self-similar subproblems.

Every recursive function needs two parts:

1. **Base Case(s):** One or more conditions that stop the recursion. Without a base case, the function would call itself forever, leading to a **stack overflow** error (the computer runs out of memory for tracking function calls).
2. **Recursive Step:** The part where the function calls itself, usually with modified arguments that move it closer to the base case.

A classic example is calculating the factorial of a non-negative integer $n$ (denoted $n!$), which is the product of all positive integers up to $n$. (0! is defined as 1). $n! = n * (n-1)!$ for $n > 0$ 0! = 1 (Base Case)

```
function factorial(n)
  -- Base case: Factorial of 0 is 1
  if n == 0 then
```

```
    return 1
  -- Recursive step: n * factorial(n-1)
  else
    return n * factorial(n - 1)
  end
end

print(factorial(5)) -- 5 * 4 * 3 * 2 * 1 = 120
-- Output: 120
print(factorial(0)) -- Output: 1
-- print(factorial(-1)) -- Error: stack overflow (no base case for negative
numbers)
```

How `factorial(3)` works:

1. `factorial(3)` calls `factorial(2)`, needs `3 * result`
2. `factorial(2)` calls `factorial(1)`, needs `2 * result`
3. `factorial(1)` calls `factorial(0)`, needs `1 * result`
4. `factorial(0)` hits the base case, returns 1.
5. `factorial(1)` receives 1, returns `1 * 1 = 1`.
6. `factorial(2)` receives 1, returns `2 * 1 = 2`.
7. `factorial(3)` receives 2, returns `3 * 2 = 6`.

Recursion can lead to elegant solutions for problems that have a naturally recursive structure (like traversing tree data structures). However, it can sometimes be less efficient (due to function call overhead) than an iterative solution using loops. Always ensure your recursive function has a clear base case!

# Chapter Summary

This chapter introduced functions, the workhorses of code organization and reuse in Lua. You learned how to define functions using `function...end`, call them with `()`, pass information using parameters and arguments, and get results back using `return`, including Lua's handy ability to return multiple values. We explored variable arguments (`...`) for flexible input. The critical concept of variable scope (`local` vs. global) was reinforced, highlighting why `local` is strongly preferred. We uncovered the power of functions as first-class values, enabling patterns like callbacks and closures – functions that remember their creation environment. Finally, we touched upon recursion as a problem-solving technique where functions call themselves.

Functions allow us to package behavior. Often, this behavior operates on data, or functions themselves are treated *as* data. The primary way to structure data in Lua is using tables. In the next chapter, we'll dive deep into tables, Lua's remarkably versatile and fundamental data structure.

# 6

# Tables

Prepare yourself for the most important, most versatile, and arguably most ingenious feature of Lua: the **table**. In many other programming languages, you have separate tools for different kinds of collections – arrays for ordered lists, dictionaries or maps for key-value lookups, maybe sets or other structures. Lua takes a radically simple approach: it provides *one* fundamental data structure, the table, which can elegantly handle all these roles and more. Understanding tables is key to mastering Lua, as they are used for everything from simple lists to complex object-oriented programming (as we'll glimpse in Chapter 15). Let's dive into how to create, manipulate, and traverse these powerful containers.

## The One Structure to Rule Them All

So, what exactly *is* a table? At its heart, a table is an **associative array**. You can think of it like a smart dictionary or a collection of labeled boxes. Each entry in a table consists of a **key** and a **value**.

- **Key:** The label or index you use to access an entry. In Lua, keys can be almost any value – numbers, strings, booleans, even other tables or functions (though nil cannot be used as a key).
- **Value:** The data stored at that key. Values can be of any Lua type, including nil (though assigning nil effectively removes the key-value pair).

This simple key-value structure allows tables to behave like:

- **Arrays/Lists:** By using consecutive positive integers (1, 2, 3, ...) as keys.
- **Dictionaries/Maps/Hashes:** By using strings or other non-integer values as keys.
- **Records/Structs:** By using descriptive string keys (like field names).
- **Objects:** By storing data (fields) and functions (methods), often combined with metatables (Chapter 7).
- **Sets:** By storing elements as keys with a dummy value (like `true`).

This unification simplifies the language immensely but requires you to understand how to use tables effectively in different contexts.

# Creating Tables

You create tables using **table constructors**, denoted by curly braces {}.

## The Empty Table

The simplest table is an empty one:

```lua
local emptyContainer = {}
print(type(emptyContainer)) -- Output: table
```

## List-Style Constructor

To create a table that acts like a list or array, you can list the values separated by commas. Lua automatically assigns positive integer keys starting from **1** (this is the standard convention in Lua – indices start at 1, not 0 like in many other languages).

```lua
local colors = { "red", "green", "blue" }
-- Equivalent to:
-- local colors = {}
-- colors[1] = "red"
-- colors[2] = "green"
-- colors[3] = "blue"

local numbers = { 10, 20, 30, 40, 50 }
```

# Record-Style Constructor

To create a table that acts like a dictionary or record, you specify key-value pairs using the syntax [key] = value or, for string keys that are valid identifiers, the shorthand key = value.

```
-- Using string keys with the shorthand syntax
local player = { name = "Alex", score = 1500, active = true }
-- Equivalent to:
-- local player = {}
-- player["name"] = "Alex"
-- player["score"] = 1500
-- player["active"] = true

-- Using other key types requires the square bracket syntax
local descriptions = {
  [1] = "First item",
  ["color"] = "Orange",
  [true] = "Boolean key associated value",
  [{}] = "Table key associated value" -- Using an empty table as a key
}
```

The key = value syntax is very common for creating dictionary-like tables with string keys.

# Mixing Styles

You can mix list-style and record-style entries within the same constructor:

```
local mixedTable = {
  "apple",                       -- Implicit key [1] = "apple"
  "banana",                      -- Implicit key [2] = "banana"
  count = 2,                     -- Explicit key ["count"] = 2
  [10] = "Something at index 10", -- Explicit key [10] = ...
  fruitType = "Tropical"         -- Explicit key ["fruitType"] = ...
}
```

Table constructors are expressions, meaning you can assign them directly to variables, pass them to functions, or return them from functions.

# Accessing Table Elements

Once you have a table, you need a way to get values out of it or put new values in. This is done by **indexing** the table using a key.

## Using Square Brackets [ ]

The fundamental way to index a table is using square brackets []. Inside the brackets, you place the key whose value you want to access or modify. This works for *any* type of key.

```lua
local colors = { "red", "green", "blue" }
local player = { name = "Alex", score = 1500 }

-- Accessing values
local firstColor = colors[1] -- Access using integer key 1
local playerName = player["name"] -- Access using string key "name"

print(firstColor)  -- Output: red
print(playerName) -- Output: Alex

-- Modifying values
colors[2] = "dark green" -- Change the value at key 2
player["score"] = player["score"] + 100 -- Update the score

print(colors[2])          -- Output: dark green
print(player["score"])     -- Output: 1600

-- Accessing with a variable key
local keyToAccess = "name"
print(player[keyToAccess]) -- Output: Alex
```

## Dot Notation .

For convenience, Lua offers **dot notation** as syntactic sugar when the key is a **string** that follows the same rules as Lua variable names (letters, numbers, underscores, not starting with a number, not a keyword).

`tableName.keyName` is exactly equivalent to `tableName["keyName"]`.

```lua
local player = { name = "Alex", score = 1500 }

-- Accessing using dot notation
```

```
local playerName = player.name
print(playerName) -- Output: Alex

-- Modifying using dot notation
player.score = player.score + 50
print(player.score) -- Output: 1550

-- Adding a new key-value pair using dot notation
player.level = 3
print(player.level) -- Output: 3
```

Dot notation is generally preferred for record-style tables because it's cleaner, but remember it **only works for valid identifier string keys**. You cannot use it for numeric keys or string keys containing spaces or special characters.

```
local myTable = {}
myTable[1] = "Numeric key"
myTable["key with spaces"] = "String key with spaces"

-- print(myTable.1) -- SYNTAX ERROR!
print(myTable[1]) -- Output: Numeric key

-- print(myTable.key with spaces) -- SYNTAX ERROR!
print(myTable["key with spaces"]) -- Output: String key with spaces
```

## What Happens When a Key Doesn't Exist?

If you try to access a key that doesn't exist in the table, Lua doesn't raise an error. Instead, it simply evaluates to `nil`.

```
local data = { value = 10 }
print(data.value)   -- Output: 10
print(data.missing) -- Output: nil
print(data[1])      -- Output: nil (key 1 doesn't exist)
```

This behavior is useful because you can use it to check for the existence of a key:

```
if data.optionalSetting == nil then
  print("Optional setting not found, using default.")
  -- Use a default value
else
  print("Using provided optional setting:", data.optionalSetting)
end
```

# Tables as Arrays (Lists/Sequences)

While tables can use any keys, a common and important use case is treating them as arrays or lists by using consecutive integer keys starting from 1.

```
local shoppingList = { "milk", "eggs", "bread" }
print(shoppingList[1]) -- Output: milk
print(shoppingList[3]) -- Output: bread
```

## Adding Elements to Sequences

A common task is adding an element to the end of a sequence. You can do this using the length operator # (which we'll discuss next) to find the next available index:

```
local tasks = { "Write report", "Attend meeting" }
print(#tasks) -- Output: 2

tasks[#tasks + 1] = "Call client" -- Add to the end (index 3)
print(tasks[3]) -- Output: Call client
print(#tasks) -- Output: 3
```

*(There's also* `table.insert`, *covered in Chapter 12, which is often clearer for this).*

## The Length Operator # Revisited

We saw the length operator # used with strings in Chapter 3. It also works with tables, but its behavior is specifically defined for tables intended to be used as **sequences** (arrays with positive integer keys starting from 1).

The # operator returns an integer key n such that t[n] is not nil and t[n+1] is nil. If the table is empty or doesn't have a positive integer key, it returns 0. Essentially, it finds the **last numerical index** in a sequence starting from 1 *without gaps*.

```
local sequence = { 10, 20, 30, 40 }
print(#sequence) -- Output: 4

local empty = {}
print(#empty) -- Output: 0

local mixed = { 10, name = "Bob", 30 }
print(#mixed) -- Output: 1 (It finds t[1] is not nil, t[2] is nil)
```

```
local sparse = { [1] = "a", [10] = "b" }
print(#sparse) -- Output might be 1 or 0 or 10 (behavior is not reliable here)
```

**Crucial Pitfall: Holes!** If your sequence has "holes" – nil values assigned to integer keys within the sequence – the behavior of # becomes **unpredictable** and might not give you the result you expect.

```
local hasHole = { "apple", "banana", nil, "orange" }
-- hasHole[1] = "apple", hasHole[2] = "banana", hasHole[3] = nil, hasHole[4] =
"orange"
print(#hasHole) -- Output: 2 (or possibly 4, depending on Lua version/details)
               -- It finds t[2] is not nil, but t[3] IS nil, so it might stop
there.
```

**Recommendation:** If you are using a table as an array/sequence and relying on the # operator, **avoid putting** nil **values inside the sequence**. If you need to remove an element, use table.remove (Chapter 12), which shifts subsequent elements to keep the sequence dense.

# Tables as Dictionaries (Maps, Associative Arrays)

The real power and flexibility of Lua tables shine when you use them as dictionaries, associating arbitrary keys with values. String keys are the most common choice here.

```
local fileInfo = {
  filename = "report.txt",
  size_kb = 128,
  type = "text/plain",
  readonly = false
}

print("File:", fileInfo.filename)
print("Size (KB):", fileInfo.size_kb)

fileInfo.readonly = true -- Modify a value
fileInfo.last_modified = os.time() -- Add a new key-value pair

print("Read only:", fileInfo.readonly)
```

You aren't limited to strings or numbers as keys. Any Lua value except `nil` (and NaN - Not a Number) can be a key:

```lua
local lookup = {}
local keyTable = { id = 1 }
local keyFunc = function() print("key") end

lookup[keyTable] = "Value associated with keyTable"
lookup[keyFunc] = "Value associated with keyFunc"
lookup[true] = "Value associated with true"

print(lookup[keyTable]) -- Output: Value associated with keyTable
print(lookup[true])     -- Output: Value associated with true
```

Using tables or functions as keys is less common than strings or numbers but demonstrates the flexibility of the underlying mechanism.

# Traveling Through Tables

How do you process *all* the elements in a table without knowing the keys beforehand? Lua provides the **generic** `for` **loop** combined with **iterator functions**.

## `pairs(t)`

The most common way to iterate over *all* entries in a table (regardless of key type) is using `pairs`. It returns an iterator function that, on each step of the generic `for` loop, provides the next key-value pair from the table.

**Important:** The order in which `pairs` visits the elements is **not specified** and can change between runs or Lua versions. Do not rely on `pairs` giving you elements in any particular order (especially not the order you defined them in!). This is because tables are internally implemented using hash tables for efficiency.

```lua
local config = {
  width = 1920,
  height = 1080,
  fullscreen = true,
  title = "Game Window"
}

print("Configuration:")
for key, value in pairs(config) do
  -- 'key' gets the key ("width", "height", etc.)
```

```
    -- 'value' gets the corresponding value (1920, 1080, etc.)
    print("  " .. tostring(key) .. ": " .. tostring(value))
end
```

**Possible Output (Order might vary!):**

```
Configuration:
  height: 1080
  width: 1920
  title: Game Window
  fullscreen: true
```

# ipairs(t)

If you specifically want to iterate over the array part of a table (keys 1, 2, 3, …) **in order**, you should use ipairs. It returns an iterator that provides the index (key) and value for integer keys 1, 2, 3, and so on, stopping at the first integer key that is not present in the table (i.e., the first "hole").

```
local days = { "Monday", "Tuesday", "Wednesday", "Thursday", "Friday" }

print("Weekdays:")
for index, dayName in ipairs(days) do
  -- 'index' gets the integer key (1, 2, 3, 4, 5)
  -- 'dayName' gets the corresponding value
  print("  Day " .. index .. ": " .. dayName)
end

local mixedSequence = { 10, 20, nil, 40, [1] = 5 } -- Note: [1]=5 overwrites the
first 10
print("\nMixed sequence with ipairs:")
for i, v in ipairs(mixedSequence) do
    print("  Index:", i, "Value:", v)
end
```

**Output:**

```
Weekdays:
  Day 1: Monday
  Day 2: Tuesday
  Day 3: Wednesday
  Day 4: Thursday
  Day 5: Friday
```

```
Mixed sequence with ipairs:
  Index: 1 Value: 5
  Index: 2 Value: 20
```

Notice how ipairs stopped at index 2 because mixedSequence[3] is nil. It didn't see the value 40 at index 4.

## Numeric for Loop with #t

For simple array iteration where you know the sequence is dense (no nil holes), you can still use the numeric for loop combined with the length operator #.

```
local scores = { 100, 95, 88, 72, 99 }
print("\nScores using numeric for:")
for i = 1, #scores do
  print(" Score " .. i .. ": " .. scores[i])
end
```

**Output:**

```
Scores using numeric for:
  Score 1: 100
  Score 2: 95
  Score 3: 88
  Score 4: 72
  Score 5: 99
```

This is often slightly more efficient than ipairs for pure array iteration, but remember the caveat about # and holes. Generally, ipairs is safer if you aren't certain the sequence is dense.

# Modifying Tables

Tables are dynamic; you can add, change, and remove elements after they've been created.

## Adding New Key-Value Pairs

Simply assign a value to a key that doesn't exist yet:

```
local person = { name = "Eva" }
person.age = 25            -- Add using dot notation
person["city"] = "London" -- Add using bracket notation
```

# Changing Existing Values

Assign a new value to an existing key. The old value is overwritten.

```
local settings = { volume = 80 }
settings.volume = 95 -- Update the value
```

# Removing Elements

To remove a key-value pair from a table, assign nil to its key. This effectively deletes the entry.

```
local inventory = { weapon = "sword", potion = 3, gold = 150 }
print(inventory.potion) -- Output: 3

inventory.potion = nil -- Remove the potion entry

print(inventory.potion) -- Output: nil
print("\nRemaining inventory (order might vary):")
for k, v in pairs(inventory) do
  print(" ", k, v)
end
```

**Output:**

```
3
nil

Remaining inventory (order might vary):
  gold 150
  weapon sword
```

Assigning nil is the *only* way to truly remove an entry from a table. Setting inventory.potion = 0 would just change the value, not remove the key itself.

# Common Table Gotchas

Tables are powerful, but there are a few points that often trip up newcomers:

1. **Keys Must Be Unique:** If you assign a value to a key that already exists, the old value is replaced. You can't have two entries with the exact same key.

2. `pairs` **vs.** `ipairs`: Remember `pairs` is for *all* keys in *unspecified order*, while `ipairs` is for the *ordered integer sequence* (1, 2, 3...). Use the right tool for the job.

3. **The # Operator and Holes/Non-Sequence Keys:** # only reliably works for sequences (arrays starting at 1 with no `nil` values in the middle). Don't use it expecting the "total number of elements" in a dictionary-like table; use a manual count with `pairs` for that if needed.

4. **Tables are Objects (Reference Types):** When you assign a table variable to another variable, you are *not* creating a copy of the table. Both variables end up pointing to the *same* table in memory. Modifying the table through one variable affects the other.

```lua
local t1 = { 10, 20 }
local t2 = t1 -- t2 now refers to the SAME table as t1

t2[1] = 99 -- Modify the table using t2

print(t1[1]) -- Output: 99 (t1 sees the change because it's the same
table)

-- To create an independent copy, you need to manually copy elements:
local t3 = {}
for k, v in pairs(t1) do
  t3[k] = v
end
t3[1] = 111
print(t1[1]) -- Output: 99 (t1 is unaffected by changes to the copy t3)
print(t3[1]) -- Output: 111
```

Understanding this reference behavior is crucial.

# Chapter Summary

Tables are the cornerstone of data structuring in Lua. In this chapter, you learned how to create them using constructors (`{}`, list-style, record-style, mixed), how to access and modify their elements using square brackets ([]) and dot notation (.), and how nil signifies a missing key. We explored using tables as both 1-based sequences (arrays) and versatile dictionaries (maps). You mastered iteration using the generic for loop with pairs (for all elements, unordered) and ipairs (for the integer sequence, ordered), and understood the specific behavior and limitations of the length operator (#). Finally, we highlighted common pitfalls like the reference nature of tables and the difference between pairs and ipairs.

Tables provide the structure, but their default behavior is quite basic. What if you wanted to define what happens when you try to add two tables together, or look up a key that doesn't exist? In the next chapter, we'll unlock a powerful customization layer for tables: **metatables**.

# 7

# Metatables

In the previous chapter, we established that tables are Lua's ultimate data structuring tool. They are incredibly flexible, acting as arrays, dictionaries, and more. But their default behavior is straightforward: you store key-value pairs, retrieve them, and that's about it. What if you wanted more? What if you could define what happens when you try to add two tables representing, say, 2D vectors? Or what if you wanted a table to automatically provide a default value when you try to access a key that doesn't exist? Lua provides a unique and elegant solution for this kind of customization: **metatables**. Think of metatables as a way to attach special instructions to a table, defining how it should behave under certain operations, effectively giving your plain tables superpowers.

## Beyond Basic Tables

Imagine you have two tables representing points in a 2D space:

```lua
local point1 = { x = 10, y = 20 }
local point2 = { x = 5,  y = 7  }
```

Wouldn't it be nice if you could just write `point1 + point2` to get a new point representing their vector sum (`{ x = 15, y = 27 }`)? If you try this in standard Lua, you'll get an error:

```
-- This causes an error:
-- local sum = point1 + point2
-- ERROR: attempt to perform arithmetic on a table value (local 'point1')
```

Lua doesn't inherently know how to add tables. Likewise, consider accessing data:

```
local defaults = { width = 800, height = 600 }
local userSettings = { height = 768 }

-- We want userSettings.width to return defaults.width if it's not set
print(userSettings.width) -- Output: nil (Default Lua behavior)
```

We want `userSettings.width` to magically fall back to `defaults.width` if it doesn't exist directly in `userSettings`.

These are the kinds of situations where metatables shine. They allow you to intercept operations like addition (+), indexing (`table[key]`), assignment (`table[key] = value`), and others, and provide your own custom logic.

## What is a Metatable?

A metatable is, quite simply, **just another Lua table**. What makes it special is its *purpose*. You associate this metatable with your original table, and Lua will look inside the metatable for specific **keys** (called **metamethods**) when certain operations are performed on the original table. The *values* associated with these metamethod keys are typically **functions** that implement the custom behavior.

Think of it like this: Your data table is the object itself. The metatable is like an instruction manual attached to that object. When Lua tries to do something unusual with the object (like adding it to another object), it checks the instruction manual (metatable) for a specific instruction (metamethod) on how to proceed.

# The `setmetatable` and `getmetatable` Functions

Lua provides two main functions for working with metatables:

1. `setmetatable(table, metatable)`: This function attaches the `metatable` (which must be a table or `nil`) to the `table`. It also returns the original `table`, allowing for chaining. If the original table already had a metatable with a

__metatable field, setmetatable will error (this is a protection mechanism, preventing easy modification of metatables others might rely on).

```lua
local myData = { value = 10 }
local myMeta = { special_instruction = "Handle with care" }

setmetatable(myData, myMeta)

-- Now 'myData' has 'myMeta' associated with it.
```

2. getmetatable(table): This function returns the metatable associated with the given table, or nil if it doesn't have one. If the metatable itself has a __metatable field, getmetatable will return the value of that field instead of the actual metatable (again, a protection mechanism).

```lua
local theMeta = getmetatable(myData)
if theMeta then
  print(theMeta.special_instruction) -- Output: Handle with care
else
  print("No metatable found.")
end
```

# Metamethods

The real magic happens inside the metatable. The keys within the metatable that Lua recognizes are called **metamethods**. These names always start with two underscores (__). When you perform an operation on a table that has a metatable, Lua checks if the metatable contains the corresponding metamethod key. If it does, Lua calls the function associated with that key (or uses the value in other ways, as we'll see with __index and __newindex).

Here are some of the most important metamethods:

# Overloading Operators

This allows you to change the meaning of standard operators when applied to your tables.

# Arithmetic Metamethods

These are called when arithmetic operators are used on tables with corresponding metamethods in their metatables. The associated value must be a function that takes two arguments (the operands) and returns the result.

- `__add(a, b)`: For the + operator.
- `__sub(a, b)`: For the - operator.
- `__mul(a, b)`: For the * operator.
- `__div(a, b)`: For the / operator.
- `__mod(a, b)`: For the % operator.
- `__pow(a, b)`: For the ^ operator.
- `__unm(a)`: For the unary - operator (negation).

**Example: Vector Addition**

```lua
local Vector = {} -- Acts as a simple 'class' or prototype for our vectors
Vector.__index = Vector -- We'll explain this shortly, needed for method calls

function Vector:new(x, y)
  local instance = { x = x, y = y }
  return setmetatable(instance, Vector) -- Attach metatable on creation
end

-- The __add metamethod function
function Vector.__add(vec1, vec2)
  -- Ensure both operands are vectors (or compatible) - check omitted for
brevity
  local newX = vec1.x + vec2.x
  local newY = vec1.y + vec2.y
  return Vector:new(newX, newY) -- Return a *new* vector
end

-- Let's add a way to print vectors nicely later: __tostring
function Vector:__tostring()
    return "Vector(" .. self.x .. ", " .. self.y .. ")"
end

local v1 = Vector:new(10, 20)
local v2 = Vector:new(5, 7)

local vSum = v1 + v2 -- Lua sees '+', finds v1's metatable, calls
Vector.__add(v1, v2)

print(vSum) -- Output: Vector(15, 27) (using the __tostring we'll add later)
```

# Relational Metamethods

These handle comparison operators. Unlike arithmetic metamethods, Lua only needs definitions for equality (__eq), less than (__lt), and less than or equal (__le). If you try a > b, Lua converts it to b < a (using __lt). If you try a >= b, it becomes b <= a (using __le). If you try a ~= b, it becomes not (a == b) (using __eq).

- __eq(a, b): For the == operator. Returns true or false. Crucially, if __eq is defined, Lua will *not* use its default reference comparison for tables; it relies solely on your function.
- __lt(a, b): For the < operator. Returns true or false.
- __le(a, b): For the <= operator. Returns true or false.

**Example: Simple Set Equality (checking if two sets have the same elements)**

```lua
-- (Assume Set is a table with elements as keys, value = true)
local SetMeta = {}
function SetMeta.__eq(set1, set2)
  -- 1. Check if sizes are different (using a hypothetical #set approach)
  -- (We'll see how to customize # using __len later)
  local size1 = 0; for _ in pairs(set1) do size1 = size1 + 1 end
  local size2 = 0; for _ in pairs(set2) do size2 = size2 + 1 end
  if size1 ~= size2 then return false end

  -- 2. Check if every element in set1 is also in set2
  for key, _ in pairs(set1) do
    if not set2[key] then -- If key from set1 is not found in set2
      return false
    end
  end
  -- (Technically don't need to check the other way due to equal sizes)
  return true
end

local s1 = { apple = true, banana = true }
setmetatable(s1, SetMeta)
local s2 = { banana = true, apple = true }
setmetatable(s2, SetMeta)
local s3 = { apple = true, cherry = true }
setmetatable(s3, SetMeta)

print(s1 == s2) -- Output: true (Calls SetMeta.__eq)
print(s1 == s3) -- Output: false (Calls SetMeta.__eq)
print(s1 == { apple = true, banana = true }) -- Output: false (The other table
has no metatable)
```

## Concatenation Metamethod

- `__concat(a, b)`: For the `..` (concatenation) operator. Usually used to define how to combine two tables (often sequences) into one.

```lua
local ListMeta = {}
function ListMeta.__concat(list1, list2)
  local newList = {}
  -- Copy elements from list1
  for i=1, #list1 do newList[#newList + 1] = list1[i] end
  -- Copy elements from list2
  for i=1, #list2 do newList[#newList + 1] = list2[i] end
  return setmetatable(newList, ListMeta) -- Return a new list
end

local l1 = { 10, 20 }
setmetatable(l1, ListMeta)
local l2 = { 30, 40, 50 }
setmetatable(l2, ListMeta)

local combined = l1 .. l2 -- Calls ListMeta.__concat(l1, l2)
print(table.concat(combined, ", ")) -- Output: 10, 20, 30, 40, 50
```

# Controlling Table Access

This is perhaps the most frequent and powerful use of metatables, defining what happens when you try to read from or write to keys that don't exist directly in the table.

## The `__index` Metamethod

When you try to access `table[key]` and `key` is **not** present in `table`, Lua checks if `table` has a metatable with an `__index` field.

There are two possibilities for the `__index` value:

1. `__index` **refers to another table:** If `metatable.__index` is itself a table, Lua will **repeat the lookup** for `key` inside *that second table*.

   ```lua
   local defaults = { background = "blue", fontsize = 12 }
   local userPrefs = { fontsize = 14 }

   -- Make userPrefs look up missing keys in 'defaults'
   setmetatable(userPrefs, { __index = defaults })
   ```

```
print(userPrefs.fontsize)     -- Output: 14 (Found directly in userPrefs)
print(userPrefs.background) -- Output: blue (Not in userPrefs, Lua
checks metatable.__index)
                            --          (It looks up "background" in the
'defaults' table)
print(userPrefs.margin)       -- Output: nil (Not in userPrefs, not in
defaults)
```

This is the fundamental mechanism used to implement **inheritance** and prototypes in Lua (a preview of Chapter 15). An "object" (like `userPrefs`) can inherit properties and methods from its "class" or "prototype" (like `defaults`).

2. `__index` **refers to a function**: If `metatable.__index` is a function, Lua calls this function with two arguments: the original table (`table`) and the key that was being accessed (`key`). The value returned by this function becomes the result of the original access `table[key]`.

```
local dataStore = {}
local meta = {}

function meta.__index(table, key)
  print(">> Accessing missing key:", key)
  if type(key) == "string" and key:sub(1, 4) == "calc" then
    -- Example: Calculate value on the fly for keys starting with "calc"
    local num = tonumber(key:sub(5)) -- Get number after "calc"
    if num then return num * 10 end
  end
  -- Otherwise, return a default value
  return "Default Value"
end

setmetatable(dataStore, meta)

dataStore.existing = 100
print(dataStore.existing) -- Output: 100 (Found directly)
print(dataStore.missing)  -- Output: >> Accessing missing key: missing
                          --            Default Value
print(dataStore.calc5)    -- Output: >> Accessing missing key: calc5
                          --            50
```

Using a function for `__index` allows for complex logic like lazy loading, calculated properties, or providing dynamic defaults.

# The __newindex Metamethod

When you try to assign a value table[key] = value and key is **not** already present in table, Lua checks if table has a metatable with a __newindex field.

Like __index, there are two possibilities:

1. __newindex **refers to another table:** If metatable.__newindex is a table, the assignment table[key] = value is **redirected** and performed on *that second table* instead of the original one. The original table remains unchanged.

   ```lua
   local original = { name = "Original" }
   local logTable = {} -- We'll store new assignments here
   local meta = { __newindex = logTable }
   setmetatable(original, meta)

   original.name = "Changed Original" -- Key "name" exists, assigns
   directly to 'original'
   original.newKey = 123           -- Key "newKey" DOESN'T exist, uses
   __newindex

                                   -- Assignment goes to 'logTable' instead

   print(original.name)   -- Output: Changed Original
   print(original.newKey) -- Output: nil (It wasn't added to 'original')

   print(logTable.newKey) -- Output: 123 (It was added to 'logTable')
   ```

2. __newindex **refers to a function:** If metatable.__newindex is a function, Lua calls this function with three arguments: the original table (table), the key being assigned (key), and the value being assigned (value). This allows you to completely control the assignment behavior.

   **Example: Read-Only Table**

   ```lua
   local readOnlyData = { config = "A" }
   local readOnlyMeta = {}

   function readOnlyMeta.__newindex(table, key, value)
     error("Attempt to modify a read-only table! Key: " .. key, 2)
     -- 'error' stops the script. The '2' tells error not to blame this
   function itself.
   end

   function readOnlyMeta.__index(table, key)
       -- Allow reading existing keys
   ```

```
    -- For this simple example, we use rawget to avoid infinite loop if
key isn't there
    return rawget(table, key)
  end

setmetatable(readOnlyData, readOnlyMeta)

print(readOnlyData.config) -- Output: A (Reading is allowed via
__index/rawget)
-- readOnlyData.config = "B" -- Allowed: Modifies existing key directly.
__newindex is NOT called for existing keys.
-- readOnlyData.newField = "C" -- ERROR! Attempt to add a new key
triggers __newindex function -> error(...)
```

*(Note: Making a table truly read-only, including preventing modification of existing keys, is slightly more complex, often involving __index and __newindex carefully combined, possibly using rawset inside __newindex if conditional writes were allowed).*

Using a function for __newindex enables validation, logging assignments, redirecting writes, or preventing writes altogether.

# Other Useful Metamethods

- __tostring(a): Called by the tostring() function (and often implicitly by print()) when applied to a table with this metamethod. Allows you to provide a custom string representation.

```
local PointMeta = {
  __tostring = function(p)
    return "Point(x=" .. p.x .. ", y=" .. p.y .. ")"
  end
}
local pt = { x = 10, y = -5 }
setmetatable(pt, PointMeta)
print(pt) -- Output: Point(x=10, y=-5)
```

- __len(a): Called when the length operator # is used on a table with this meta-method. Lets you define what "length" means for your custom table type.

```
local MySetMeta = {
  __len = function(set)
```

```
      local count = 0
      for _ in pairs(set) do count = count + 1 end
      return count
    end
  }
  local mySet = { apple = true, orange = true }
  setmetatable(mySet, MySetMeta)
  print(#mySet) -- Output: 2 (Calls MySetMeta.__len)
```

- __call(a, ...): Allows a table to be called as if it were a function. The first argument to the metamethod function is the table itself, followed by any arguments passed in the call.

```
local multiplierMeta = {
  __call = function(obj, value)
    return value * obj.factor
  end
}
local doubler = { factor = 2 }
setmetatable(doubler, multiplierMeta)
local tripler = { factor = 3 }
setmetatable(tripler, multiplierMeta)

print(doubler(10)) -- Output: 20 (Calls multiplierMeta.__call(doubler,
10))
print(tripler(10)) -- Output: 30 (Calls multiplierMeta.__call(tripler,
10))
```

# Metatables in Action

Let's combine a few metamethods to create a basic Set data type.

```
local Set = {}
Set.__index = Set -- For potential future methods

-- Metatable for Set instances
local SetMeta = {
  __index = Set, -- Inherit methods from 'Set' table

  -- Union of two sets using '+'
  __add = function(set1, set2)
    local union = Set:new() -- Create a new empty set
    for k in pairs(set1) do union:add(k) end
```

```lua
    for k in pairs(set2) do union:add(k) end
    return union
  end,

  -- Nice string representation
  __tostring = function(set)
    local items = {}
    for k in pairs(set) do items[#items + 1] = tostring(k) end
    table.sort(items) -- For consistent output order
    return "{" .. table.concat(items, ", ") .. "}"
  end,

  -- Calculate size using '#'
  __len = function(set)
    local count = 0
    for _ in pairs(set) do count = count + 1 end
    return count
  end
}

-- Constructor function for sets
function Set:new(initialElements)
  local instance = {} -- The actual set data (keys are elements)
  setmetatable(instance, SetMeta)
  if initialElements then
    for _, element in ipairs(initialElements) do
      instance[element] = true -- Store element as key
    end
  end
  return instance
end

-- Method to add an element
function Set:add(element)
  self[element] = true
end

-- Method to check membership
function Set:has(element)
  return self[element] == true
end


-- Usage
local s1 = Set:new({ "apple", "banana" })
local s2 = Set:new({ "banana", "orange" })
```

```
s1:add("cherry")

print("Set 1:", s1)                          -- Output: Set 1: {apple, banana, cherry}
print("Set 2:", s2)                          -- Output: Set 2: {banana, orange}
print("Does s1 have apple?", s1:has("apple")) -- Output: Does s1 have apple?
true
print("Size of s1:", #s1)                    -- Output: Size of s1: 3

local unionSet = s1 + s2                      -- Uses __add
print("Union:", unionSet)                    -- Output: Union: {apple, banana, cherry,
orange}
print("Size of union:", #unionSet) -- Output: Size of union: 4
```

This example shows how metamethods (__add, __tostring, __len) combined with regular functions attached via __index (like Set:new, Set:add, Set:has) allow us to create a custom data type with its own behavior using standard Lua tables.

# Chapter Summary

Metatables are Lua's mechanism for providing customized behavior for tables (and userdata). They are themselves just tables containing special keys called metamethods (like __add, __index, __newindex, __tostring, __len, __call, etc.). By setting a metatable for a table using setmetatable, you can intercept operations like arithmetic, comparisons, concatenation, table indexing (reading and writing missing keys), length calculation, string conversion, and even function calls, defining your own logic via the associated metamethod functions. This powerful feature enables operator overloading, inheritance patterns (using __index), data validation, default values, read-only tables, and the creation of rich, object-like structures within Lua's fundamentally simple framework.

You now have a deep understanding of Lua's core data structure, the table, and how to tailor its behavior with metatables. Next, we'll shift our focus back to another fundamental data type: strings, exploring Lua's built-in library for powerful text manipulation and pattern matching.

*8*

# Mastering Text

Text is everywhere in the digital world. From user interfaces and configuration files to log messages and data exchange formats, manipulating sequences of characters – **strings** – is a fundamental programming task. In Chapter 2, you learned the basics of creating string values. Now, we'll delve into Lua's built-in `string` **library**, a comprehensive toolkit packed with functions for searching, extracting, replacing, formatting, and analyzing text. Mastering these tools will allow you to handle textual data effectively and efficiently in your Lua programs.

## Strings Revisited

Before diving into the library, let's quickly recap some key aspects of Lua strings:

- **Literals:** You create string constants (literals) using either single quotes (`'...'`) or double quotes (`"..."`). They are equivalent, giving you the flexibility to include one type of quote inside a string delimited by the other without needing special escapes.

  ```
  local single = 'Contains "double" quotes.'
  local double = "Contains 'single' quotes."
  ```

- **Long Strings:** For strings spanning multiple lines or containing lots of quotes without needing escapes, use long brackets `[[...]]`. You can add equals signs between the brackets ([=[...]=], [===[...]===]) to allow the string itself to contain ]] sequences.

```lua
local html = [[
<html>
  <head><title>My Page</title></head>
  <body>Hello, world!</body>
</html>
]]
```

- **Escape Sequences:** Within single- or double-quoted strings, the backslash (\) acts as an escape character, allowing you to include special characters:
    - \n: Newline
    - \t: Horizontal tab
    - \\: Backslash itself
    - \": Double quote
    - \': Single quote
    - \ddd: Character with decimal code ddd (e.g., \65 is 'A')
    - \xHH: Character with hexadecimal code HH (e.g., \x41 is 'A')
    - \z: Skips following whitespace (Lua 5.3+) - useful for formatting long strings.

```lua
local formatted = "Line 1\n\tIndented Line 2\nPath: C:\\Temp"
print(formatted)
-- Output:
-- Line 1
--          Indented Line 2
-- Path: C:\Temp
```

- **Immutability:** This is crucial! Once a string is created in Lua, its content **cannot be changed**. Functions that appear to modify a string, like replacing a character or concatenating, actually create and return a *new* string, leaving the original untouched.

```lua
local original = "Hello"
local upper = string.upper(original) -- Creates a NEW string

print(original) -- Output: Hello (Original is unchanged)
print(upper)    -- Output: HELLO
```

# The `string` Library

Most string manipulation functions are conveniently grouped within the built-in string table. To use them, you typically prefix the function name with `string.`.

```
local text = "Lua is neat!"
local len = string.len(text) -- Call the 'len' function from the 'string'
library
print(len) -- Output: 12
```

Some functions, like `tostring` and `type`, are global, and operators like `#` (length) and `..` (concatenation) also work directly on strings.

# Basic String Operations

Let's start with some fundamental manipulations.

## Finding Length

As seen before, you can get the number of *bytes* in a string `s` using either the `string.len()` function or the length operator `#`. For simple ASCII strings, bytes correspond to characters.

```
local name = "Lua"
print(string.len(name)) -- Output: 3
print(#name)            -- Output: 3 (Usually preferred for brevity)
```

*(Remember the* `utf8` *library from Chapter 12 for correct character counting in UTF-8 encoded strings).*

## Repeating Strings

Creates a new string by repeating string `s` exactly `n` times. An optional separator string `sep` (Lua 5.3+) can be placed between repetitions.

```
local line = string.rep("-", 20) -- Repeat '-' 20 times
print(line) -- Output: --------------------

local pattern = string.rep("xo", 5)
print(pattern) -- Output: xoxoxoxoxo
```

```
local words = string.rep("hi", 3, ", ") -- Lua 5.3+
print(words) -- Output: hi, hi, hi
```

# Changing Case

These functions return a *new* string with all uppercase letters converted to lowercase
(string.lower) or all lowercase letters converted to uppercase (string.upper),
respectively. Non-alphabetic characters are unaffected.

```
local mixedCase = "Hello World"
local lowerCase = string.lower(mixedCase)
local upperCase = string.upper(mixedCase)

print(lowerCase) -- Output: hello world
print(upperCase) -- Output: HELLO WORLD
```

# Extracting Substrings

This function extracts and returns a portion (substring) of the string s.

- i: The starting position (1-based index).
- j (Optional): The ending position (inclusive). If omitted, it defaults to -1,
  which means "until the end of the string".

Negative indices count from the *end* of the string: -1 is the last character, -2 is the
second-to-last, and so on.

```
local text = "Programming in Lua"

local sub1 = string.sub(text, 1, 11) -- Characters 1 through 11
print(sub1) -- Output: Programming

local sub2 = string.sub(text, 16) -- Characters 16 through the end
print(sub2) -- Output: Lua

local sub3 = string.sub(text, -3) -- Last 3 characters
print(sub3) -- Output: Lua

local sub4 = string.sub(text, 1, -5) -- Characters 1 through the 5th from the
end
print(sub4) -- Output: Programming in
```

If i is greater than j, or if the indices are out of bounds in a way that defines an empty region, `string.sub` returns an empty string "".

## Reversing Strings

Returns a new string with the order of characters (bytes) in s reversed.

```
local forward = "desserts"
local backward = string.reverse(forward)
print(backward) -- Output: stressed
```

# Finding and Replacing Text

These functions allow you to search for patterns within strings and replace them.

## Finding Substrings

Searches for the first occurrence of `pattern` within the string s.

- s: The string to search within.
- `pattern`: The string (or Lua pattern, see later) to search for.
- `init` (Optional): The position in s where the search should start (defaults to 1). Can be negative.
- `plain` (Optional): If `true`, performs a plain substring search, disabling Lua's pattern matching features for the `pattern`. Defaults to `false`.

**Return Values:**

- If the pattern is found, it returns the **starting index** and **ending index** of the first match.
- If the pattern is not found, it returns `nil`.

```
local text = "The quick brown fox jumps over the lazy dog."

local startIdx, endIdx = string.find(text, "fox")
if startIdx then
  print("Found 'fox' from index " .. startIdx .. " to " .. endIdx)
  -- Output: Found 'fox' from index 17 to 19
else
  print("'fox' not found.")
end
```

```
local startThe, endThe = string.find(text, "the", 1, true) -- Plain search
print("Found 'the' (plain):", startThe) -- Output: Found 'the' (plain): 31

local startThePattern, endThePattern = string.find(text, "the") -- Pattern
search
print("Found 'the' (pattern):", startThePattern) -- Output: Found 'the'
(pattern): 31
-- (In this simple case, plain and pattern are the same)

local startTheAgain, endTheAgain = string.find(text, "the", 35) -- Start
searching from index 35
print("Found 'the' after 35:", startTheAgain) -- Output: Found 'the' after 35:
nil

local missing = string.find(text, "cat")
print("Found 'cat':", missing) -- Output: Found 'cat': nil
```

# Replacing Substrings

Performs a **global sub**stitution, returning a *new* string where occurrences of `pattern` in s are replaced by `replacement`. It also returns the total number of substitutions made.

- s: The original string.
- pattern: The string or Lua pattern to search for.
- replacement: What to replace the pattern with. This can be:
  - A **string**: Replaces the matched text. Can contain capture references like %1, %2 (see patterns later) to insert parts of the matched text. %0 refers to the whole match. %% inserts a literal %.
  - A **table**: The matched text is used as a key to look up the replacement value in this table.
  - A **function**: This function is called for each match, with the matched text (and any captures) passed as arguments. The value returned by the function is used as the replacement.
- n (Optional): Limits the maximum number of substitutions to perform. If omitted, all occurrences are replaced.

```
local text = "Hello world, hello Lua!"

-- Simple string replacement
local newText1, count1 = string.gsub(text, "hello", "Goodbye") -- Case-sensitive
print(newText1, count1) -- Output: Hello world, Goodbye Lua!        1
```

```
local newText2, count2 = string.gsub(string.lower(text), "hello", "Goodbye")
print(newText2, count2) -- Output: goodbye world, goodbye lua!    2

-- Using captures (%1 refers to the first captured group 'world' or 'lua')
local newText3, count3 = string.gsub(text, "(world|Lua)", "%1!")
print(newText3, count3) -- Output: Hello world!, hello Lua!!    2

-- Using a replacement table
local replacements = { apple = "orange", banana = "grape" }
local fruitText = "I like apple and banana."
local newFruit, count4 = string.gsub(fruitText, "%a+", replacements) -- %a+
matches words
print(newFruit, count4) -- Output: I like orange and grape.    2

-- Using a replacement function (convert matched numbers to hex)
local data = "Values: 10, 255, 128"
local function decToHex(match)
  return string.format("0x%X", tonumber(match))
end
local hexData, count5 = string.gsub(data, "%d+", decToHex) -- %d+ matches
numbers
print(hexData, count5) -- Output: Values: 0xA, 0xFF, 0x80    3

-- Limit substitutions
local limitedText, count6 = string.gsub(text, "l", "*", 3) -- Replace only first
3 'l's
print(limitedText, count6) -- Output: He**o wor*d, hello Lua!    3
```

`string.gsub` is incredibly versatile due to its powerful `replacement` options.

# Formatting Strings for Output

Often, you need to construct strings with variables embedded in them in a specific format (e.g., aligning numbers, setting decimal places). `string.format` is Lua's tool for this, inspired by the `printf` function in C.

`string.format(formatstring, ...)` takes a **format string** and a variable number of additional arguments. The format string contains literal text mixed with **format specifiers** (starting with %). Each specifier corresponds to one of the additional arguments and defines how that argument should be converted to text and inserted.

Common Format Specifiers:

- %s: String argument.

- %d: Integer argument (decimal).
- %f: Floating-point argument (standard decimal notation).
- %e, %E: Floating-point argument (scientific notation).
- %g, %G: Floating-point argument (uses shorter of %f or %e).
- %c: Integer argument, converted to the corresponding character byte.
- %q: String argument, formatted as a safely quoted Lua string literal (useful for debugging or generating code).
- %%: A literal percent sign (%).

You can add modifiers between the % and the letter for width, alignment, precision, etc.:

- -: Left-align within the specified width.
- width: Minimum field width (pads with spaces).
- .precision: For floats, number of digits after decimal point; for strings, maximum length.

```
local name = "Alice"
local score = 12345
local average = 88.7512
local item = "potion"

local s1 = string.format("Player: %s, Score: %d", name, score)
print(s1) -- Output: Player: Alice, Score: 12345

-- Formatting numbers
local s2 = string.format("Score: %06d", score) -- Pad with leading zeros to
width 6
print(s2) -- Output: Score: 012345

local s3 = string.format("Average: %.2f", average) -- 2 decimal places
print(s3) -- Output: Average: 88.75

local s4 = string.format("Avg (width 10): %10.2f", average) -- Width 10, right-
aligned
print(s4) -- Output: Avg (width 10):      88.75

local s5 = string.format("Avg (width 10, left): %-10.2f", average) -- Width 10,
left-aligned
print(s5) -- Output: Avg (width 10, left): 88.75

-- Quoting a string safely
local s6 = string.format("Item name: %q", "A 'quoted' string\nwith newline")
print(s6) -- Output: Item name: "A 'quoted' string\nwith newline"
```

```
local s7 = string.format("Percentage: 50%%") -- Literal %
print(s7) -- Output: Percentage: 50%
```

string.format is essential for creating nicely formatted output for users or logs.

# Working with Individual Characters

Sometimes you need to deal with the underlying numerical codes of characters.

## Getting Character Codes

Returns the internal numerical codes (usually ASCII or byte values in UTF-8) of the characters in string s.

- i (Optional): Starting position (defaults to 1).
- j (Optional): Ending position (defaults to i).

It returns one number per character requested.

```
local code_H = string.byte("Hello", 1) -- Code of first character 'H'
print(code_H) -- Output: 72 (ASCII code for 'H')

local code_e, code_l, code_l = string.byte("Hello", 2, 4) -- Codes for 'e', 'l',
'l'
print(code_e, code_l) -- Output: 101   108 (only prints first two returned
values here)
print(string.byte("Hello", -1)) -- Code of last character 'o'
-- Output: 111
```

## Creating Strings from Codes

Does the reverse of string.byte. Takes zero or more integer arguments and returns a new string composed of the characters corresponding to those numerical codes.

```
local str = string.char(72, 101, 108, 108, 111) -- Codes for H, e, l, l, o
print(str) -- Output: Hello

local abc = string.char(string.byte("A"), string.byte("B"), string.byte("C"))
print(abc) -- Output: ABC
```

# Powerful Pattern Matching

This is one of the most powerful parts of Lua's string library. Lua provides its own **pattern matching** system, which is similar in concept to regular expressions (regex) found in other languages but with a simpler syntax and slightly different features. Patterns allow you to describe sequences of characters in a flexible way, going far beyond simple substring searching.

## Lua's Patterns vs. Regular Expressions

- **Simpler Syntax:** Lua patterns are generally less complex than full regex (e.g., no explicit OR operator | within groups, simpler quantifiers).
- **Focus on Text:** Designed primarily for text manipulation, not necessarily complex validation.
- **Integrated:** Built directly into the string library functions (`find`, `gsub`, `match`, `gmatch`).

## Understanding Pattern Syntax

Patterns are strings containing special characters and sequences:

- **Character Classes:** Represent sets of characters:
    - %a: Letters (alphabetic)
    - %d: Digits (numeric)
    - %s: Space characters (space, tab, newline, etc.)
    - %w: Alphanumeric characters (%a + %d)
    - %l: Lowercase letters
    - %u: Uppercase letters
    - %p: Punctuation characters
    - %c: Control characters
    - %x: Hexadecimal digits
    - . (Dot): Matches *any* single character.
    - [set]: Matches any character within the set (e.g., [aeiou] matches a vowel, [0-9] matches a digit, [a-zA-Z] matches any letter). Ranges are allowed.
    - [^set]: Matches any character *not* within the set (e.g., [^%s] matches any non-space character).
    - You can use %a, %d, etc. inside [] (e.g., [%w_] matches alphanumeric or underscore).

- **Anchors:** Match positions, not characters:

  - ^: Matches the beginning of the subject string (or line in multi-line mode, which isn't default).
  - $: Matches the end of the subject string (or line).

- **Quantifiers (Repetition):** Specify how many times the preceding item can occur:

  - *: Matches 0 or more occurrences (greedy - matches as many as possible).
  - +: Matches 1 or more occurrences (greedy).
  - -: Matches 0 or more occurrences (non-greedy/lazy - matches as few as possible). *This is a key difference from regex where *? is lazy.*
  - ?: Matches 0 or 1 occurrence.

- **Captures:** Parentheses () create capture groups. The text matched by the pattern inside the parentheses is "captured" and can be retrieved later (by `string.match`, `string.gmatch`, or referenced in the replacement string of `string.gsub` using %1, %2, etc.).

- **Magic Characters & Escaping:** The characters ( ) . % + - * ? [ ] ^ $ have special meanings within patterns. To match one of these characters literally, you must escape it with a percent sign % (e.g., %. matches a literal dot, %% matches a literal percent sign).

- **Special Patterns:**

  - %bxy: Matches a "balanced" pair of characters x and y. Useful for finding content within parentheses, brackets, etc. E.g., %b() matches from an opening parenthesis to its corresponding closing parenthesis.

# Using Patterns Effectively

- `string.match(s, pattern, [init])`: Searches for the *first* match of `pattern` in s (starting at `init`).

  - If the pattern has **no captures**, returns the entire matched substring.
  - If the pattern **has captures**, returns the captured substrings as separate string values.
  - If no match is found, returns `nil`.

```
local text = "Name: Alice, Age: 30, City: London"
```

```
-- No captures: find the first number
local firstNum = string.match(text, "%d+")
print(firstNum) -- Output: 30

-- With captures: extract name and age
local name, age = string.match(text, "Name: (%a+), Age: (%d+)")
print("Name:", name, "Age:", age) -- Output: Name: Alice   Age: 30

-- Capture content within parentheses
local data = "Process(Status=OK, ID=123)"
local content = string.match(data, "%b()") -- Matches '()' and captures
inner content
print(content) -- Output: (Status=OK, ID=123)
```

- `string.gmatch(s, pattern)`: Returns an **iterator function** that, each time it's called (typically in a generic `for` loop), finds the *next* match of `pattern` in `s`.

    - If the pattern has **no captures**, the iterator yields the entire matched substring on each iteration.
    - If the pattern **has captures**, the iterator yields the captured substrings as separate values on each iteration.

```
local text = "Items: apple 10, banana 5, cherry 20"

-- Iterate over all words
print("Words:")
for word in string.gmatch(text, "%a+") do
  print(" ", word)
end

-- Iterate over item names and quantities (captures)
print("\nItems and Quantities:")
for item, quantity in string.gmatch(text, "(%a+) (%d+)") do
  print("  Item:", item, "Quantity:", quantity)
end
```

### Output:

```
Words:
  Items
  apple
  banana
  cherry
```

```
Items and Quantities:
    Item: apple      Quantity: 10
    Item: banana     Quantity: 5
    Item: cherry     Quantity: 20
```

Lua patterns are a powerful tool for text processing. Experimenting with them (`string.match` is great for testing) is the best way to become proficient.

# Chapter Summary

In this chapter, you've explored Lua's comprehensive `string` library. We reviewed string basics like literals and immutability. You learned essential functions for finding length (`string.len`, `#`), repeating (`string.rep`), changing case (`string.lower`, `string.upper`), extracting substrings (`string.sub`), and reversing (`string.reverse`). We covered searching with `string.find` and the versatile `string.gsub` for replacements using strings, tables, or functions. You saw how `string.format` creates precisely formatted strings using specifiers. We touched on converting between characters and their byte codes with `string.byte` and `string.char`. Finally, you were introduced to Lua's powerful pattern matching system, understanding its syntax (character classes, quantifiers, anchors, captures, escapes) and how to use it effectively with `string.match` (for the first match/captures) and `string.gmatch` (for iterating over all matches/captures).

Working with strings and external data often involves situations where things might not go as planned – invalid input, files not found, network errors. Knowing how to anticipate and handle these situations gracefully is crucial for robust programs. In the next chapter, we'll learn about Lua's mechanisms for error handling.

# 9

# Handling the Unexpected

So far, we've been writing Lua code assuming everything goes according to plan. Numbers add up, strings concatenate, tables get indexed correctly. But the real world is messy! Users might enter invalid data, files might be missing, network connections could drop, or we might simply make a logical mistake in our code (like dividing by zero or trying to access part of a table that doesn't exist, as discussed in Chapters 3 and 6). When these unexpected things happen, Lua generates an **error**. By default, an error abruptly stops your script's execution and prints an error message. While this tells you *something* went wrong, it's often not the user-friendly or robust behavior you want. This chapter explores how Lua handles errors and, more importantly, how *you* can handle them gracefully using tools like `pcall`, `xpcall`, `error`, and `assert`, making your programs more reliable and resilient.

## When Things Go Wrong

Errors in programming generally fall into a few categories:

1. **Syntax Errors:** These are mistakes in the way you've written the code itself – like typos in keywords (`funtion` instead of `function`), missing `end` statements, or incorrect operator usage. Lua catches these *before* your script even starts running, usually when it first tries to load or compile the code. You must fix these syntax errors before the program can run at all.

```
-- Syntax error example (missing 'end')
local function greet(name)
  print("Hello, " .. name)
-- oops! forgot the 'end' here

-- Lua will likely report an error like:
-- file.lua:X: 'end' expected (to close 'function' at line Y) near <eof>
```

2. **Runtime Errors:** These errors occur *while* the program is running. They happen when the code is syntactically correct, but an operation cannot be performed legally. Examples include:

   - Trying to perform arithmetic on a non-numeric value (e.g., `10 + "hello"`).
   - Trying to call a value that isn't a function (e.g., `local x = 10; x()`).
   - Trying to index a field in a `nil` value (e.g., `local t = nil; print(t.field)`).
   - Calling `error()` explicitly (see later).

   These are the errors we primarily focus on handling programmatically, as they often depend on external factors or unpredictable program states.

3. **Logical Errors:** These are often the trickiest. The program runs without crashing (no syntax or runtime errors), but it doesn't produce the *correct* result because the logic you wrote is flawed. For example, using < instead of > in a comparison, calculating a value incorrectly, or forgetting to update a variable in a loop. Error handling mechanisms don't usually catch logical errors directly; these require careful debugging, testing (Chapter 17), and thinking through your code's logic.

This chapter focuses mainly on detecting and managing **runtime errors**.

# Catching Errors

What if you anticipate that a piece of code *might* cause a runtime error, but you don't want it to crash your whole program? For instance, you're calling a function from a third-party module that could potentially fail, or you're performing a calculation based on user input that might be invalid. Lua provides `pcall` (protected call) for exactly this scenario.

# The `pcall(func, arg1, ...)` Function

`pcall` executes a given function (`func`) in **protected mode**. This means if any runtime error occurs *during the execution of* `func`, `pcall` catches the error and prevents it from stopping the main script.

- `func`: The function you want to call safely.
- `arg1, ...`: Any arguments you want to pass to `func`.

**Return Values:** `pcall` always returns at least one value: a boolean indicating success or failure.

- **On Success:** `pcall` returns `true` followed by any values returned by `func`.
- **On Failure:** `pcall` returns `false` followed by the error object (usually the error message string).

```lua
-- A function that might cause an error
function riskyDivision(a, b)
  if b == 0 then
    error("Division by zero!") -- Explicitly raise an error
  end
  return a / b
end


-- --- Success Case ---
local status, result = pcall(riskyDivision, 10, 2)

if status then
  print("Success! Result:", result)
else
  print("Failure! Error:", result) -- Note: 'result' holds the error message
here
end
-- Output: Success! Result: 5.0


-- --- Failure Case ---
local status2, errorMsg = pcall(riskyDivision, 10, 0)

if status2 then
  print("Success! Result:", errorMsg)
else
  print("Failure! Error:", errorMsg)
end
-- Output: Failure! Error: ...file.lua:4: Division by zero!
-- (Error message includes file and line number where 'error' was called)
```

```
-- --- Another Failure Case (indexing nil) ---
local function accessNil()
    local data = nil
    return data.field -- This will cause a runtime error
end

local status3, errorMsg3 = pcall(accessNil)
if not status3 then
    print("Caught error:", errorMsg3)
    -- Output: Caught error: ...file.lua:X: attempt to index a nil value (local
'data')
end
```

pcall is your go-to tool for handling operations that are outside your direct control or known to be potentially problematic (like interacting with external systems, processing potentially malformed input, etc.).

# The xpcall(func, errhandler) Function

xpcall is similar to pcall but provides an additional capability: you can specify your own **error handler function**. If an error occurs during the execution of func, Lua calls errhandler *before* the execution stack is unwound, passing the original error object to it. The value returned by errhandler then becomes the second return value of xpcall (after false).

- func: The function to call in protected mode.
- errhandler: The function to call if an error occurs within func.

This is useful if you want to perform custom logging, add more context to the error message, or inspect the program state (using the debug library, for example) right when the error happens.

```
function functionThatFails()
  error("Something went wrong inside!")
end

function myErrorHandler(originalError)
  print("--- Custom Error Handler ---")
  print("Original Error:", originalError)
  -- Let's add more info, like a stack trace (see debug library later)
  local traceback = debug.traceback("Stack trace:", 2) -- Level 2 to skip xpcall
& handler
  return "Handled Error: " .. originalError .. "\n" .. traceback
end
```

```
-- Call functionThatFails using xpcall and our handler
local status, resultOrProcessedError = xpcall(functionThatFails, myErrorHandler)

if status then
  print("xpcall Success:", resultOrProcessedError)
else
  print("xpcall Failure! Processed Error below:")
  print(resultOrProcessedError)
end
```

**Output:**

```
--- Custom Error Handler ---
Original Error: ...file.lua:2: Something went wrong inside!
xpcall Failure! Processed Error below:
Handled Error: ...file.lua:2: Something went wrong inside!
Stack trace:
...file.lua:2: in function 'functionThatFails'
[C]: in function 'xpcall'
...file.lua:14: in main chunk
[C]: in ?
```

xpcall gives you more control over error reporting when an error is caught.

# Generating Errors Intentionally

Sometimes, *your* code detects a situation that shouldn't happen – invalid input that bypasses earlier checks, an impossible internal state, or failure to acquire a necessary resource. In these cases, you might want to deliberately stop execution and signal an error yourself. Lua provides error() and assert() for this.

## The error(message, [level]) Function

Calling error() immediately stops execution and generates (or *raises*, or *throws*) a runtime error.

- message: A string (or any value, typically a string) describing the problem. This message is what pcall or xpcall will receive if they catch the error.
- level (Optional integer): This controls where the error message indicates the error occurred in the call stack.
    - level = 1 (Default): Error location is where error() was called.

- level = 2: Error location is where the function that *called* the function containing error() was called.
- level = 0: Skips adding location information.

Usually, you use level = 1 (the default) or level = 2 if you are writing a utility function that checks arguments for *other* functions and want the error blamed on the caller of your utility.

```
function checkPositive(value, argName)
  if type(value) ~= "number" or value <= 0 then
    -- Blame the function that called checkPositive
    error("Bad argument #" .. argName .. ": positive number expected, got " ..
type(value), 2)
  end
end

function processData(dataValue)
  checkPositive(dataValue, 1) -- Check the first argument ('dataValue')
  -- ... process dataValue ...
  print("Processing successful with value:", dataValue)
end

processData(10) -- Output: Processing successful with value: 10
-- processData(-5) -- ERROR: ...file.lua:9: Bad argument #1: positive number
expected, got number
-- (Error points to line 9, where processData was called, because we used level
2)
-- processData("hello") -- ERROR: ...file.lua:9: Bad argument #1: positive
number expected, got string
```

# The assert(condition, [message]) Function

assert provides a concise way to check if a condition is true and raise an error if it's not. It's commonly used for sanity checks, verifying function arguments (preconditions), or checking results (postconditions).

- condition: The value or expression to check. Remember Lua's truthiness: only false and nil fail the assertion.
- message (Optional): The error message to use if the condition is false or nil. If omitted, assert provides a generic message like "assertion failed!".

**Behavior:**

- If condition is **true** (any value other than `false` or `nil`), assert does nothing except return all its arguments starting from the condition itself.
- If condition is **false** or `nil`, assert calls `error()` internally, passing the message (or the default message).

```lua
function divideAssert(a, b)
  assert(type(a) == "number", "Argument #1 must be a number")
  assert(type(b) == "number", "Argument #2 must be a number")
  assert(b ~= 0, "Cannot divide by zero") -- Check precondition
  local result = a / b
  -- assert(result > 0, "Result should be positive") -- Example postcondition
check
  return result
end

print(divideAssert(10, 2))    -- Output: 5.0
-- print(divideAssert(10, 0))    -- ERROR: ...file.lua:4: Cannot divide by zero
-- print(divideAssert("ten", 2)) -- ERROR: ...file.lua:2: Argument #1 must be a
number

-- Assert can return values on success
local val = assert(divideAssert(20, 4), "Division failed unexpectedly")
print("Assert returned:", val) -- Output: Assert returned: 5.0
```

assert is often preferred over `if condition then error(...)` end for its conciseness when checking essential conditions.

# Debugging

Error handling helps your program survive errors, but you still need to *find* and *fix* the underlying bugs.

- **Read the Error Message!** Lua's error messages are usually informative. They typically tell you:
  - The file name and line number where the error occurred.
  - A description of the error (e.g., "attempt to index a nil value", "attempt to perform arithmetic on...", or the message you provided to `error`/`assert`).
- **Understand Stack Traces:** When an error occurs inside nested function calls, Lua often provides a **stack trace**. This shows the sequence of function calls that led to the error, starting from the point of the error and going back up the call chain. This is invaluable for understanding the context in which the

error happened. `debug.traceback()` (used in the `xpcall` example) generates these traces.

- `print` **Debugging**: The simplest debugging technique is often just adding `print` statements to your code to check the values of variables at different points, helping you pinpoint where things start to go wrong. `print(type(variable))` is also useful.
- **Debug Library** (`debug.traceback`, **etc.**): As mentioned, `debug.traceback()` is useful for getting stack information programmatically, often within an error handler. The `debug` library (more in Chapter 12) offers more powerful introspection tools, but they are generally used for building debuggers rather than in everyday code.
- **External Debuggers**: For more complex debugging, dedicated tools or IDE plugins (like those for ZeroBrane Studio, VS Code, etc.) allow you to set breakpoints (pause execution at specific lines), step through code line-by-line, and inspect variable values interactively.

# Best Practices for Error Handling

- `pcall` **for the Unpredictable**: Use `pcall` (or `xpcall`) when dealing with operations that might fail due to external factors you can't fully control: interacting with the OS (file I/O, network calls), parsing user input, calling potentially unstable third-party code.
- `assert` **for Sanity Checks**: Use `assert` to validate internal assumptions, preconditions, and postconditions within your own code. If an `assert` fails, it usually indicates a bug in your own logic that needs fixing, not just graceful handling.
- **Clear Error Messages**: When using `error` or `assert`, provide messages that clearly explain *what* went wrong and ideally *why* (e.g., "Invalid input for 'age': expected number between 0 and 120, got -5").
- **Validate Input Early**: Check user input or data from external sources as soon as it enters your system. Don't pass potentially invalid data deep into your program's logic.
- **Resource Cleanup**: If your code acquires resources (like opening files with `io.open` - Chapter 12), ensure those resources are released (e.g., `file:close()`) even if an error occurs *after* acquiring them. `pcall` can be used around blocks that use resources, with cleanup code executed after the `pcall` regardless of success or failure. (Metatable finalizers (`__gc` - Chapter 13) can also help with automatic cleanup in some cases).

# Chapter Summary

This chapter equipped you with the knowledge to handle runtime errors in Lua. You learned to differentiate error types and focused on runtime errors. We explored how to safely execute potentially failing code using `pcall` and `xpcall`, understanding their return values and how `xpcall` allows custom error handlers. You also learned how to generate errors intentionally within your own code using `error()` for critical failures and `assert()` for concise validation of conditions. We briefly touched upon debugging strategies like interpreting error messages, stack traces, and using print statements. Finally, we discussed best practices for deciding when and how to use these error handling tools effectively.

Handling errors robustly is essential for building reliable applications. As applications grow, managing complexity also involves organizing the code itself into logical units. In the next chapter, we'll explore Lua's module system, which allows you to break your code into reusable files and manage dependencies cleanly.

# 10

# Organizing Your Code

As you've built increasingly complex programs through the previous chapters, you might have noticed your script files getting longer and potentially harder to navigate. Putting hundreds or thousands of lines of code, including functions, variables, and control structures, all into one single file quickly becomes unwieldy. It's like trying to build a house using only one giant, undifferentiated pile of materials instead of organizing them into walls, rooms, and floors. Lua provides a clean and effective solution for this: **modules**. Modules allow you to break your code into separate, self-contained files, each focused on a specific piece of functionality. This chapter will teach you how to create and use these modules, leveraging Lua's `require` function to build well-structured, maintainable, and reusable codebases.

## The Need for Structure

Why is putting everything in one file a problem?

- **Readability Suffers:** Finding a specific function or piece of logic in a massive file becomes a chore.
- **Maintenance Becomes Difficult:** Changing one part of the code might unintentionally break another part if everything is tightly interwoven. Fixing bugs requires searching through the entire file.

- **Reusability is Limited:** If you write a useful set of functions in one project file, using them in another project means copying and pasting, leading to duplication and potential inconsistencies if you update the original.
- **Collaboration is Harder:** Multiple people working on the same large file simultaneously often leads to conflicts and confusion.
- **Name Clashes:** Without careful use of `local` (as emphasized in Chapter 5), global variables defined in one part of the file can easily clash with those defined elsewhere.

**Modules** address these issues by promoting:

- **Organization:** Code related to a specific task (e.g., player management, file utilities, UI rendering) is grouped into its own file.
- **Reusability:** A well-designed module can be easily used (`required`) in multiple projects.
- **Encapsulation / Name Spacing:** Modules typically only expose a specific set of functions and variables (their public interface), hiding internal implementation details. This prevents accidental modification from outside and significantly reduces the chance of global name collisions.
- **Easier Collaboration:** Different team members can work on different modules more independently.

# What is a Lua Module?

In modern Lua, the standard convention for creating a module is remarkably simple:

1. **A Lua module is typically a standard Lua file (`.lua`).**
2. **Inside the module file, you define functions and variables, preferably using the `local` keyword** to keep them private to the module by default.
3. **You create a table (often named `M` or something descriptive by convention) within the module file.**
4. **You add the functions and variables that you want to make** *public* **(accessible from outside the module) as fields to this table.**
5. **At the very end of the module file, you `return` this table.**

This returned table *is* the module from the perspective of the code that uses it. It acts as a container or namespace for the module's public functionality.

# Creating a Simple Module

Let's create a basic module for simple string utility functions.

1. Create a new file named strutils.lua.
2. Add the following code to strutils.lua:

```lua
-- strutils.lua
-- A simple module for string utilities

-- Create the table that will be returned as the module's interface
local M = {}

-- Internal helper function (not exposed publicly)
local function isValidString(s)
  return type(s) == "string"
end

-- Public function: Check if a string is empty or nil
function M.isEmpty(s)
  return s == nil or s == ""
end

-- Public function: Repeat a string N times
-- (We already have string.rep, but this is for illustration)
function M.repeatString(s, n)
  if not isValidString(s) or type(n) ~= "number" or n < 0 then
    -- Using error discussed in Chapter 9
    error("Invalid arguments for repeatString", 2)
  end
  local result = ""
  for i = 1, n do
    result = result .. s
  end
  return result
end

-- Public variable (less common, but possible)
M.version = "1.0"

-- Return the public interface table
return M
```

Key points in this example:

- local M = {}: We create a local table M to hold our public interface.

- `local function isValidString...`: This helper function is `local` and *not* added to M, so it cannot be called directly from outside the module. It's an implementation detail.
- `function M.isEmpty...` and `function M.repeatString...`: These functions are added as fields to the M table using dot notation. They become part of the public interface.
- `M.version = "1.0"`: We can also add variables to the public interface.
- `return M`: The crucial last step that makes the M table available to code that requires this module.

# Using Modules

Now that we have our `strutils.lua` module, how do we use it in another Lua file (say, `main.lua`)? We use the built-in `require` function.

`require` takes a single argument: a string representing the **module name**. By convention, this is usually the filename *without* the `.lua` extension.

1. Create a file named `main.lua` in the **same directory** as `strutils.lua`.
2. Add the following code to `main.lua`:

```
-- main.lua
-- A script that uses the strutils module

-- Use 'require' to load the module.
-- The returned table (M from strutils.lua) is stored in the local variable
'strutils'.
local strutils = require("strutils")

-- Now we can call the public functions using the variable name:
local name = ""
if strutils.isEmpty(name) then
  print("Name is empty.")
end

local separator = strutils.repeatString("=", 10)
print(separator)

print("String Utilities Version:", strutils.version)

-- Trying to access the internal function will fail:
-- print(strutils.isValidString) -- This would print 'nil'
-- strutils.isValidString("test") -- This would cause an error (attempt to call
a nil value)
```

```
-- Trying to require it again:
print("\nRequiring again...")
local strutils_again = require("strutils")

-- Check if it's the exact same table (it should be!)
if strutils == strutils_again then
  print("require returned the same cached table.")
end
```

Run main.lua from your terminal:

```
lua main.lua
```

**Output:**

```
Name is empty.
==========
String Utilities Version: 1.0

Requiring again...
require returned the same cached table.
```

**How require Works:**

1. **Search:** require("modname") looks for a file that can provide the module "modname". It searches through a specific list of paths defined in package.path (more on this next). It typically looks for modname.lua.
2. **Check Cache:** Before loading, require checks if the module "modname" has *already* been loaded by looking in the package.loaded table.
3. **Load and Execute (if not cached):** If the module isn't cached, require finds the corresponding file (e.g., strutils.lua), loads it, and executes its Lua code from top to bottom.
4. **Cache Result:** require takes the value returned by the module file (in our case, the M table) and stores it in package.loaded["modname"].
5. **Return Value:** require returns the value retrieved from the cache (either newly stored or found in step 2).

Because require caches the result, a module's code is only executed **once**, no matter how many times you require it in your project. Subsequent calls simply return the already-loaded module table, ensuring efficiency and preventing side effects from running multiple times.

# Understanding `package.path`

How does `require` know where to look for `strutils.lua`? It uses a search path string stored in `package.path`. This is just a regular Lua string containing a sequence of **templates**, separated by semicolons (;). Each template tells `require` where to look for a file, using a question mark (?) as a placeholder for the module name.

You can see your system's default path by printing it:

```
print(package.path)
```

The output will vary depending on your operating system and Lua installation, but it might look something like this (simplified):

- **Linux/macOS:**          `./?.lua;./?/init.lua;/usr/local/share/lua/5.4/?.lua;/usr/local/share/lua/5.4/?/init.lua;...`
- **Windows:**          `.\?.lua;.\?\init.lua;C:\Program    Files\Lua\5.4\lua\?.lua;C:\Program Files\Lua\5.4\lua\?\init.lua;...`

When you call `require("strutils")`:

1. Lua replaces ? in the first template (`./?.lua`) with "strutils", resulting in `./strutils.lua`.
2. It checks if a file exists at that path relative to the current directory (`.`). If found, it loads it.
3. If not found, it tries the next template (`./?/init.lua`), looking for `./strutils/init.lua`.
4. It continues this process through all templates in `package.path` until it finds a matching file or exhausts the path (in which case `require` raises an error).

The `?/init.lua` pattern is used for "packages" containing multiple modules (see next section).

Usually, you don't need to modify `package.path` directly. Placing your module files in the same directory as the script that requires them, or in subdirectories, often works because `./?.lua` (current directory) is typically included early in the path. For larger projects or shared libraries, you might set the LUA_PATH environment variable before running Lua, which prepends its value to the default `package.path`.

# Packages

As projects grow, even organizing code into individual module files might not be enough. You might want to group related modules together. This is where **packages** come in. A package isn't a special construct in Lua; it's simply a convention for organizing modules using directories.

Imagine you're building a small game and want to separate drawing utilities from physics calculations. You could create a directory structure like this:

```
mygame/
├── main.lua
├── engine/
│   ├── init.lua       (Optional main entry point for the 'engine' package)
│   ├── draw.lua       (Drawing functions)
│   └── physics.lua    (Physics calculations)
└── utils/
    └── string_helpers.lua
```

To use modules from these subdirectories in `main.lua`, you use a dot (.) in the `require` string to represent the directory separator:

```lua
-- main.lua

-- Require the drawing module from the 'engine' directory
local draw = require("engine.draw")

-- Require the physics module
local physics = require("engine.physics")

-- Require the string helpers
local stringHelpers = require("utils.string_helpers")

-- You *could* also potentially require the 'engine' package itself
-- if engine/init.lua exists and returns something useful.
-- local engineCore = require("engine")

draw.rectangle(10, 10, 50, 30)
local pos = physics.updatePosition({x=0, y=0}, {dx=1, dy=2}, 0.1)
local formatted = stringHelpers.trim("  extra spaces  ")
```

When Lua sees `require("engine.draw")`, it replaces the . with the appropriate directory separator (like / or \) when trying the templates in `package.path`. For example, using the template `./?.lua`, it would look for `./engine/draw.lua`. Using `./?/init.lua`, it would look for `./engine/draw/init.lua`.

This directory-based organization makes managing larger collections of related modules much cleaner.

# The `package` **Library**

Lua provides a global `package` table that holds information and functions related to module loading. We've already encountered some parts:

- `package.path`: The search path string for Lua modules.

- `package.loaded`: A table used by `require` to cache loaded modules. Keys are the module names (e.g., `"strutils"`, `"engine.draw"`), and values are the results returned by the module files (usually the module tables). You can inspect this table to see what's loaded.

  ```
  local strutils = require("strutils")
  print(package.loaded["strutils"] == strutils) -- Output: true
  ```

- `package.preload`: A table where you can manually register "loader functions" for specific module names *before* `require` searches `package.path`. When `require("modname")` is called, if `package.preload["modname"]` exists and is a function, `require` calls this function instead of searching the file system. This is useful for embedding modules directly into your script or loading them from non-standard sources.

  ```
  -- Pre-register a loader for a virtual module 'virtual_mod'
  package.preload["virtual_mod"] = function()
    print("Loading virtual_mod...")
    local M = {}
    M.greet = function() print("Hello from virtual module!") end
    return M
  end

  local vm = require("virtual_mod") -- Executes the preload function
  vm.greet()
  -- Output:
  -- Loading virtual_mod...
  -- Hello from virtual module!
  ```

- package.cpath: Similar to `package.path`, but this is the search path used by `require` when looking for **C libraries** (dynamic-link libraries like `.so`, `.dll`). We'll touch on C integration in Chapter 14.

# An Older Approach

In older Lua code (pre-Lua 5.1, though it lingered), you might encounter a different way of defining modules using a global `module()` function:

```
-- oldstyle_module.lua (DON'T WRITE NEW CODE LIKE THIS)
module("oldstyle_module", package.seeall)

-- Functions defined here become GLOBAL by default within the module's
environment
function greet()
  print("Hello from oldstyle_module!")
end

-- Variables also become global within the module unless marked local
version = "0.1"
```

Using this module would involve:

```
-- main_using_oldstyle.lua
require("oldstyle_module")

-- Functions/variables from the module are accessed directly as globals
oldstyle_module.greet()
print(oldstyle_module.version)
```

The `module(...)` function did some complex setup behind the scenes, creating an environment table for the module and often making global variables inside the module appear as fields of a global table named after the module. `package.seeall` was often used to grant the module access to existing global variables.

**Why is this approach now discouraged and the `require`/table-return pattern preferred?**

- **Global Pollution:** The `module()` function inherently relied on creating global variables (the module table itself, and potentially its contents if not careful), increasing the risk of name clashes.

- **Implicit Exports:** It wasn't always immediately clear which functions/variables were intended to be public. Anything not explicitly `local` could become part of the module's table or environment.
- **Less Clear Dependencies:** The `package.seeall` option made it harder to track which external globals a module depended on.
- **Complexity:** The environment manipulation done by `module()` was more complex than the straightforward table-returning approach.

The modern `local M = {}; ...; return M` pattern combined with `local myMod = require("myMod")` is much more explicit, cleaner, avoids global namespace pollution, and is the standard practice in the vast majority of current Lua projects. Stick to this pattern!

## Module Design Tips

- **Keep Modules Focused:** Aim for modules that do one thing well (or handle one specific area of concern). This follows the Single Responsibility Principle and makes modules easier to understand, test, and reuse.
- **Minimize Dependencies:** If possible, design modules to have few dependencies on other modules. This reduces coupling and makes your overall system more flexible.
- **Export Only What's Necessary:** Use `local` for all internal helper functions and variables. Only add functions/variables to the returned module table that are truly part of the module's public Application Programming Interface (API).
- **Clear Naming:** Choose clear, descriptive names for your module files (e.g., `json_parser.lua`, `network_utils.lua`) and the functions/variables within their public interface.
- **Consistency:** Use a consistent convention for naming the module table inside the file (e.g., always `local M = {}`) and for naming functions (e.g., `camelCase` or `snake_case`).

## Chapter Summary

In this chapter, you learned the essential technique for organizing Lua code into manageable units: **modules**. We explored the standard pattern of creating a module as a Lua file that defines local functions/variables, populates a table with its public interface, and returns that table. You learned how to load and use these modules using the `require` function, understanding its caching mechanism and how it uses pack-

`age.path` to find files. We also covered how to structure related modules into packages using directories and dots (.) in `require` strings. While briefly mentioning the older `module()` function, we emphasized why the modern table-returning approach is superior. Finally, we discussed best practices for designing clean, reusable, and maintainable modules.

Organizing code with modules is crucial for scalability. Sometimes, within a module or across modules, you need parts of your program to manage tasks that seem to run concurrently, pausing and resuming without blocking the entire application. Lua provides a unique and lightweight mechanism for this called **coroutines**, which we will explore in the next chapter.

# 11

# Cooperative Multitasking

In Chapter 10, we learned how to structure larger Lua projects using modules, organizing related code into separate files. This helps manage complexity from a structural perspective. However, sometimes the complexity lies in the flow of execution itself. Imagine needing to handle multiple network connections concurrently, reading data from a large file piece by piece without loading it all into memory, or implementing complex character AI in a game where different behaviors need to pause and resume.

Traditional operating system threads can handle concurrency, but they often come with significant overhead and complexities related to synchronization (preventing multiple threads from interfering with shared data). Lua offers a different, remarkably lightweight, and elegant solution called **coroutines**. Coroutines provide a mechanism for *cooperative multitasking*, allowing you to write concurrent tasks that explicitly yield control to one another, all running within a single OS thread.

## What Are Coroutines?

Think of a coroutine as a function that has the ability to pause its execution at certain points and then resume later, exactly where it left off. Unlike regular functions, which run until they return or error, coroutines can voluntarily suspend themselves using `coroutine.yield()` and be reactivated later using `coroutine.resume()`.

Key characteristics of Lua coroutines:

1. **Not True Parallel Threads:** This is crucial. All coroutines within a standard Lua program run sequentially within the *same* operating system thread. Only one coroutine is executing at any given moment. They provide concurrency (managing multiple logical tasks over time) but not parallelism (multiple tasks executing simultaneously on different CPU cores).
2. **Cooperative Multitasking:** Coroutines decide for themselves when to pause (yield). They cooperate by explicitly giving up control. This contrasts with *preemptive* multitasking (used by OS threads), where the operating system decides when to interrupt one thread and switch to another, whether the thread likes it or not.
3. **Lightweight:** Creating and managing coroutines is very efficient in Lua. You can have thousands or even tens of thousands of coroutines running without the heavy memory and context-switching overhead associated with OS threads.
4. **Resume/Yield Data Transfer:** Coroutines can send data back to the resuming function when they yield, and the resuming function can send data back into the coroutine when it resumes. This allows for powerful two-way communication.

Think of it like players in a turn-based board game. Each player (coroutine) takes their turn (runs) until they decide their turn is over (yield). Then, control passes to the next player (another coroutine is resumed).

# The `coroutine` Library

Lua provides a standard library table named `coroutine` containing the functions needed to create and manage coroutines.

# Creating and Running Coroutines

## `coroutine.create(func)`

This function creates a new coroutine based on the Lua function `func`. It doesn't start the coroutine; it just packages the function into a coroutine object and returns it. The type of this object is `"thread"`.

```lua
local function myCoroutineTask()
  print("Coroutine: Starting task...")
  coroutine.yield() -- Pause execution here
```

```
  print("Coroutine: Resuming task...")
  print("Coroutine: Task finished.")
end

-- Create the coroutine, but don't run it yet
local co = coroutine.create(myCoroutineTask)

print("Coroutine type:", type(co))      -- Output: Coroutine type: thread
print("Coroutine status:", coroutine.status(co)) -- Output: Coroutine status:
suspended
```

# coroutine.resume(co, arg1, ...)

This function starts or resumes the execution of the coroutine co.

- co: The coroutine object returned by coroutine.create.
- arg1, ...: Any arguments to pass *into* the coroutine.
  - On the **first** call to resume, these arguments are passed as parameters to the coroutine's main function (myCoroutineTask in the example).
  - On **subsequent** calls to resume, these arguments become the **return values** of the coroutine.yield() call that previously suspended the coroutine.

**Return Values:** coroutine.resume always returns a boolean status first.

- **On Success (Coroutine yields or finishes normally):** Returns true followed by any arguments passed to coroutine.yield() (if it yielded) or any values returned by the coroutine function (if it finished).
- **On Failure (Error inside the coroutine):** Returns false followed by the error message or error object.

Let's resume the coroutine we created:

```
print("\nResuming coroutine for the first time:")
local success, yield_result1 = coroutine.resume(co)
print("Resume status:", success)
print("Value from yield:", yield_result1) -- Will be nil as yield() had no args
print("Coroutine status after yield:", coroutine.status(co))

print("\nResuming coroutine again (passing a value):")
local success2, final_result = coroutine.resume(co, "Data from main")
print("Resume status:", success2)
```

```
-- 'final_result' would hold return values if the task function returned
anything
print("Coroutine status after finish:", coroutine.status(co))

print("\nTrying to resume a finished coroutine:")
local success3, errorMsg = coroutine.resume(co)
print("Resume status:", success3)
print("Error message:", errorMsg)
```

**Output:**

```
Coroutine type: thread
Coroutine status: suspended

Resuming coroutine for the first time:
Coroutine: Starting task...
Resume status: true
Value from yield:        nil
Coroutine status after yield: suspended

Resuming coroutine again (passing a value):
Coroutine: Resuming task...
Coroutine: Task finished.
Resume status: true
Coroutine status after finish: dead

Trying to resume a finished coroutine:
Resume status: false
Error message: cannot resume dead coroutine
```

# Pausing Execution

## coroutine.yield(val1, ...)

This function is called *from within* a running coroutine to suspend its execution.

- val1, ...: Any values the coroutine wants to pass back to the function that called coroutine.resume. These become the results returned by resume (after the initial true status).

Crucially, when the coroutine is later resumed (via another call to coroutine.resume), the coroutine.yield function call itself will **return** the arguments that were passed to that resume call.

Let's modify our example to show this data exchange:

```lua
local function dataExchangeTask(initialArg)
  print("Coroutine: Started with argument:", initialArg)

  -- Yield, sending a value back to the resumer
  local resumeArg1 = coroutine.yield("Coroutine needs data")
  print("Coroutine: Resumed with argument:", resumeArg1)

  -- Yield again, sending another value
  local resumeArg2 = coroutine.yield("Coroutine finished processing step 1")
  print("Coroutine: Resumed with argument:", resumeArg2)

  return "Task Complete!" -- Final return value
end

local co = coroutine.create(dataExchangeTask)

print("--- First Resume ---")
local status1, yieldVal1 = coroutine.resume(co, "Initial Value")
print("Main: Status:", status1, "Yielded:", yieldVal1)
print("Main: Coroutine status:", coroutine.status(co))

print("\n--- Second Resume ---")
local status2, yieldVal2 = coroutine.resume(co, "Data Packet A")
print("Main: Status:", status2, "Yielded:", yieldVal2)
print("Main: Coroutine status:", coroutine.status(co))

print("\n--- Third Resume ---")
local status3, finalReturn = coroutine.resume(co, "Data Packet B")
print("Main: Status:", status3, "Final Return:", finalReturn)
print("Main: Coroutine status:", coroutine.status(co))
```

**Output:**

```
--- First Resume ---
Coroutine: Started with argument:      Initial Value
Main: Status:    true    Yielded:      Coroutine needs data
Main: Coroutine status: suspended

--- Second Resume ---
Coroutine: Resumed with argument:       Data Packet A
Main: Status:    true    Yielded:      Coroutine finished processing step 1
Main: Coroutine status: suspended

--- Third Resume ---
Coroutine: Resumed with argument:       Data Packet B
```

```
Main: Status:    true    Final Return:    Task Complete!
Main: Coroutine status: dead
```

This shows the back-and-forth communication clearly.

# Checking the State

## coroutine.status(co)

As seen in the examples, this function returns a string indicating the current state of coroutine co:

- "running": The coroutine is currently executing (this can only be true for the coroutine that *calls* status on itself).
- "suspended": The coroutine is paused (either freshly created, or after calling yield).
- "normal": The coroutine is active but not the one currently running (i.e., it resumed another coroutine). This status is less commonly encountered directly.
- "dead": The coroutine has finished executing its main function (either normally or due to an unhandled error caught by resume). Dead coroutines cannot be resumed again.

# A Simpler Way

Managing the resume/yield cycle explicitly can sometimes be verbose, especially for simpler cases like iterators. coroutine.wrap provides a convenient alternative.

coroutine.wrap(func) creates a coroutine from func, just like coroutine.create, but instead of returning the coroutine object, it returns a **new function**. Calling this new function effectively calls coroutine.resume on the hidden coroutine.

- Arguments passed to the wrapped function are passed to resume.
- Values yielded by the coroutine are returned by the wrapped function call.
- If the coroutine raises an error, the error is propagated by the wrapped function call (it's not caught like with resume).

**Example: Simple Generator using wrap**

```lua
local function countUpTo(n)
  print("Counter coroutine starting...")
  for i = 1, n do
    coroutine.yield(i) -- Yield the next number
  end
  print("Counter coroutine finished.")
  -- No explicit return needed for this generator style
end

-- Create the wrapped function (the generator)
local nextNumber = coroutine.wrap(countUpTo)

print("Calling generator for n=3:")
print("Got:", nextNumber(3)) -- First call passes '3' as argument to countUpTo
print("Got:", nextNumber()) -- Subsequent calls resume
print("Got:", nextNumber())
-- The next call will finish the loop and potentially cause an error if called
again
-- depending on how the wrapped function handles the end of the coroutine.
-- Let's try calling it again after it should be finished:
print("Got:", nextNumber()) -- This might return nil or error depending on Lua
version/context

-- Let's re-run to show it finishing within the loop
local nextNumber2 = coroutine.wrap(countUpTo)
print("\nCalling generator for n=2:")
for i=1, 3 do -- try to get 3 numbers
    local num = nextNumber2(2) -- argument '2' only matters on first call
    if num == nil then
        print("Generator finished at iteration", i)
        break
    end
    print("Got:", num)
end
```

## Output:

```
Calling generator for n=3:
Counter coroutine starting...
Got:    1
Got:    2
Got:    3
Counter coroutine finished.
Got:    nil -- Example: Lua 5.4 returns nil after the coroutine finishes

Calling generator for n=2:
```

```
Counter coroutine starting...
Got:    1
Got:    2
Counter coroutine finished.
Generator finished at iteration 3
```

`coroutine.wrap` is often much cleaner when the primary purpose is to create an iterator or generator function.

# Common Use Cases for Coroutines

Coroutines excel in scenarios involving cooperative, sequential tasks that need to pause and resume.

1.  **Iterators / Generators:** As seen with `coroutine.wrap`, they are perfect for creating functions that generate a sequence of values one at a time, yielding each value as needed. This avoids generating the entire sequence upfront, saving memory (e.g., reading lines from a huge file).
2.  **Simulating Asynchronous Operations:** In environments like game engines or web servers that handle non-blocking I/O (input/output), coroutines allow you to write asynchronous code in a more synchronous style. For example, you might request data from a network, `yield` the coroutine, and the event loop resumes the coroutine later when the data arrives. This avoids deeply nested callbacks ("callback hell").
3.  **State Machines:** Implementing complex logic flows (like AI behavior or UI interaction sequences) where the entity progresses through different states, potentially pausing in each state to wait for events or time to pass. Coroutines naturally model these pauses and transitions.
4.  **Producer/Consumer Pattern:** One coroutine (the producer) generates data items and `yields` them. Another coroutine (the consumer) `resumes` the producer to get the next item, processes it, and then `resumes` the producer again. This allows data to flow between them without requiring large intermediate buffers.

# Coroutines vs. Operating System Threads

It's vital to reiterate the difference:

| Feature | Lua Coroutines | OS Threads |
|---------|----------------|------------|
| Scheduling | Cooperative (explicit `yield`) | Preemptive (OS decides) |
| Parallelism | None (single OS thread) | Potential true CPU parallelism |
| Resource Cost | Very Low | Higher (memory, context switch) |
| Data Sharing | Simpler (usually no locks needed) | Complex (requires locks, mutexes) |
| CPU-Bound Tasks | Not suitable for speedup | Can speed up on multi-core CPUs |

Use coroutines for managing concurrent *logical* tasks, asynchronous operations, and complex stateful flows within a single thread. Use OS threads (often via external libraries or the Lua C API) when you need true parallel execution to speed up CPU-intensive computations on multi-core processors.

# Chapter Summary

In this chapter, you've delved into Lua's cooperative multitasking feature: coroutines. You learned that they are functions capable of being suspended with `coroutine.yield` and resumed with `coroutine.resume`, facilitating data exchange during these transitions. We covered how to create them with `coroutine.create`, check their status with `coroutine.status`, and use the convenient `coroutine.wrap` function to create iterator-like functions. We explored common use cases like generators, asynchronous simulation, state machines, and the producer-consumer pattern. Critically, we distinguished cooperative coroutines running in a single OS thread from preemptive OS threads capable of true parallelism.

Coroutines are a sophisticated tool in your Lua arsenal. They are part of Lua's standard library, which provides many other useful tools for common tasks. In the next chapter, we'll take a tour of these standard libraries, exploring built-in capabilities for math, operating system interaction, file I/O, debugging, and more.

# 12

# Exploring Lua's Built-in Tools

Lua's core language, with its variables, control structures, functions, and tables, is remarkably simple and elegant. However, real-world programs need to perform tasks beyond basic computation – they need to calculate trigonometry, interact with the operating system, read and write files, manipulate data structures efficiently, and sometimes even peek under the hood for debugging. Lua doesn't burden its core with all this functionality; instead, it provides a collection of **standard libraries**, which are pre-built modules automatically available in any standard Lua environment. These libraries give you ready-to-use tools for a wide range of common tasks, saving you from having to write them yourself. This chapter takes you on a guided tour of the most important standard libraries, showcasing the power and convenience they offer.

## The Power of Included Libraries

Think of the Lua core language as a basic workshop with essential tools like hammers and screwdrivers. The standard libraries are like specialized toolkits placed on the shelves – a trigonometry kit, a file-handling kit, a system-interaction kit. You don't *have* to use them, but they are there when you need them, vastly extending what you can build without requiring you to install anything extra. Learning what's available in these libraries prevents you from "reinventing the wheel" and allows you to leverage efficient, well-tested implementations provided by the Lua creators themselves.

We've already encountered some standard libraries implicitly: the `string` library (Chapter 8) provided functions like `string.gsub`, and the `coroutine` library (Chapter 11) gave us `coroutine.create` and `coroutine.yield`. Now, let's explore the others.

# Mathematical Muscle

The `math` library provides a standard collection of mathematical functions and constants. If you need to do more than basic arithmetic, this library is your friend.

- **Trigonometric Functions:** Operate in *radians*, not degrees!
  - `math.sin(rad)`, `math.cos(rad)`, `math.tan(rad)`
  - `math.asin(val)`, `math.acos(val)`, `math.atan(val)`
  - `math.atan2(y, x)` (Calculates atan(y/x), handling signs correctly to find the quadrant)
  - `math.rad(deg)`: Converts degrees to radians.
  - `math.deg(rad)`: Converts radians to degrees.

```
local angle_deg = 45
local angle_rad = math.rad(angle_deg)
print(string.format("Sine of %d degrees is %.4f", angle_deg,
math.sin(angle_rad)))
-- Output: Sine of 45 degrees is 0.7071
```

- **Logarithms and Exponentials:**
  - `math.exp(x)`: Returns $e^x$.
  - `math.log(x, [base])`: Returns the logarithm of x. If base is omitted, it's the natural logarithm (base $e$); otherwise, it's $\log_{base}(x)$. (Base argument added in Lua 5.2+). `math.log10(x)` is available in Lua 5.1 for base 10.
  - `math.sqrt(x)`: Returns the square root of x (equivalent to `x ^ 0.5`).
- **Rounding and Integer/Fractional Parts:**
  - `math.floor(x)`: Returns the largest integer less than or equal to x (rounds down).
  - `math.ceil(x)`: Returns the smallest integer greater than or equal to x (rounds up).

- `math.modf(x)`: Returns two values: the integer part of x and the fractional part of x.

```
print(math.floor(3.9)) -- Output: 3
print(math.ceil(3.1))  -- Output: 4
local intPart, fracPart = math.modf(-2.7)
print(intPart, fracPart) -- Output: -2      -0.7
```

- **Constants:**

  - `math.pi`: The value of π (approximately 3.14159...).
  - `math.huge`: A value representing "infinity" (larger than any representable number). Useful for comparisons.

- **Random Numbers:**

  - `math.randomseed(n)`: Initializes the pseudo-random number generator using n as a seed. Call this *once* at the start of your program (e.g., `math.randomseed(os.time())`) for less predictable sequences.
  - `math.random([m [, n]])`: Generates pseudo-random numbers.
    - Called without arguments: Returns a float between 0.0 (inclusive) and 1.0 (exclusive).
    - Called with one integer argument m: Returns an integer between 1 and m (inclusive).
    - Called with two integer arguments m and n: Returns an integer between m and n (inclusive).

```
math.randomseed(os.time()) -- Seed the generator (using os.time, see
next section)

print(math.random())       -- Output: (A random float like 0.723...)
print(math.random(6))      -- Output: (A random integer 1-6, like a die
roll)
print(math.random(10, 20)) -- Output: (A random integer 10-20)
```

- **Min/Max and Absolute Value:**

  - `math.min(x, ...)`: Returns the minimum value among its arguments.
  - `math.max(x, ...)`: Returns the maximum value among its arguments.
  - `math.abs(x)`: Returns the absolute value of x.

- **Other Utilities (Lua 5.3+):** Includes `math.type(x)` (returns `"integer"`, `"float"`, or `nil`), `math.tointeger(x)` (converts to integer if possible), `math.ult(m, n)` (unsigned less than comparison).

# Interacting with the System

The `os` library provides functions for interacting with the underlying operating system, covering time, files, environment variables, and executing commands. Its capabilities can vary slightly depending on the OS Lua is running on.

- **Time and Date:**
    - `os.time([table])`: Returns the current time as a timestamp (usually seconds since the epoch - Jan 1, 1970). If passed a table with fields `year`, `month`, `day`, `hour`, `min`, `sec`, `isdst`, it converts that date/time into a timestamp.
    - `os.date([format [, time]])`: Formats a timestamp (`time`, defaults to current time) into a human-readable string according to the `format` string (similar to C's `strftime`). If `format` starts with `!`, it formats in UTC; otherwise, it uses the local timezone. If `format` is `"*t"`, it returns a table containing the date/time components (`year`, `month`, `day`, etc.).

```
local currentTime = os.time()
print("Timestamp:", currentTime) -- Output: Timestamp: (a large integer
like 1678886400)

-- Format current time
local dateStr = os.date("%Y-%m-%d %H:%M:%S") -- ISO-like format
print("Current Date/Time:", dateStr) -- Output: Current Date/Time: 2023-
03-15 14:00:00 (example)

-- Get date components as a table
local dateTable = os.date("*t", currentTime)
print("Year:", dateTable.year, "Month:", dateTable.month, "Day:",
dateTable.day)
-- Output: Year: 2023 Month: 3 Day: 15 (example)
```

- `os.clock()`: Returns the approximate CPU time used by the program in seconds (as a float). Useful for basic benchmarking.

```
local start_cpu = os.clock()
-- Perform some intensive calculation here...
```

```
local duration = os.clock() - start_cpu
print(string.format("Calculation took %.4f CPU seconds", duration))
```

- os.difftime(t2, t1): Returns the difference in seconds between two timestamps t2 and t1.
- **File System Operations:** These directly interact with the OS file system. Be careful!

    - os.rename(oldname, newname): Renames a file or directory. Returns true on success, nil + error message on failure.
    - os.remove(filename): Deletes a file. Returns true on success, nil + error message on failure.
    - os.execute([command]): Executes an operating system shell command. Returns a status code (often 0 for success, non-zero for failure, but OS-dependent). If called without arguments, returns true if a shell is available. *Use with extreme caution*, especially with user-provided input, as it can be a security risk.

    ```
    -- Example: Check if a file exists (using rename trick - not ideal,
    io.open is better)
    -- local success, err = os.rename("myfile.txt", "myfile.txt")
    -- if success then print("File exists") else print("File doesn't exist
    or error:", err) end

    -- Example: List files in current directory (OS-dependent command)
    -- print("Executing 'ls' or 'dir':")
    -- os.execute(package.config:sub(1,1) == '\\' and 'dir' or 'ls') --
    Basic OS detection
    ```

- **Environment:**

    - os.getenv(varname): Returns the value of an environment variable varname, or nil if it's not defined.
    - os.setlocale(locale [, category]) (Lua 5.3+): Sets the current locale for specific categories (like number formatting, time formatting).
- **Exiting and Temporary Files:**

    - os.exit([code [, close]]): Terminates the host program. code is usually 0 for success, non-zero for error. If close is true (Lua 5.2+), it attempts to close the Lua state cleanly (running finalizers).
    - os.tmpname(): Returns a string containing a filename suitable for a temporary file. *Note: This just provides a name; it doesn't create the file.*

# Reading and Writing

The io library provides functions for input and output operations, primarily focused on reading from and writing to files or the standard input/output streams.

- **Default Streams:** Lua maintains default input and output streams. Initially, these are usually the program's standard input (keyboard) and standard output (console).

  - io.input([file]): Sets the default input stream to file (an open file handle or filename). Called without arguments, returns the current default input stream handle.
  - io.output([file]): Sets the default output stream. Called without arguments, returns the current default output stream handle.
  - io.read(...): Reads data from the *default* input stream according to specified formats (see below).
  - io.write(...): Writes its arguments to the *default* output stream (similar to print, but with less formatting - no tabs between arguments, no automatic newline).

- **Working with Files Explicitly (Preferred):** It's generally better practice to work with specific file handles rather than relying on the default streams.

  - **Opening Files:** io.open(filename [, mode])

    - Opens the file specified by filename in the given mode.
    - Returns a **file handle** object on success, or nil + error message on failure.
    - Common modes:
      - "r": Read mode (default).
      - "w": Write mode (overwrites existing file or creates new).
      - "a": Append mode (writes to end or creates new).
      - "r+": Read/update mode (file must exist).
      - "w+": Write/update mode (overwrites or creates).
      - "a+": Append/update mode (writes to end or creates).
      - Append b (e.g., "rb", "wb+") for binary mode (important on Windows to prevent newline translation).

```
local file, err = io.open("mydata.txt", "w") -- Open for writing
if not file then
  print("Error opening file:", err)
```

```
      return -- Exit if opening failed
    end
```

- **Closing Files:** `file:close()` or `io.close(file)`

  - Closes the file handle `file`, flushing any buffered output.
  - It's **crucial** to close files you open, especially those opened for writing, to ensure all data is saved and resources are released. Using `file:close()` is the idiomatic object-oriented style. Returns `true` on success, or `nil` + error on failure.

```
-- ... write to file ...
local success, close_err = file:close()
if not success then
  print("Error closing file:", close_err)
end
```

*(Tip: Use* `pcall` *around file operations and ensure* `close` *is called even if errors occur within the block).*

- **Reading from Files:** `file:read(...)`

  - Reads data from the file handle `file` according to formats. Same formats as `io.read`:
    - `"*n"`: Reads a number.
    - `"*a"`: Reads the whole file from the current position.
    - `"*l"`: Reads the next line (without the newline character).
    - `"*L"`: Reads the next line (including the newline character).
    - `number`: Reads a string with up to `number` bytes.
  - Returns the read data, or `nil` on end-of-file.

```
local infile, err = io.open("config.txt", "r")
if infile then
  local firstLine = infile:read("*l")
  print("First line:", firstLine)
  local restOfFile = infile:read("*a")
  print("Rest of file:", restOfFile)
  infile:close()
end
```

- **Writing to Files:** `file:write(...)`

  - Writes its arguments (which should be strings or numbers) to the file handle `file`. Returns the file handle on success, `nil` + error on failure.

```lua
local outfile, err = io.open("log.txt", "a") -- Append mode
if outfile then
  outfile:write(os.date(), " - Program started.\n")
  outfile:write("Processed item: ", tostring(someItem), "\n")
  outfile:close()
end
```

- **Iterating Over Lines:** `file:lines(...)`

  - Returns an iterator function (for use in a generic `for` loop) that reads the file line by line. Accepts the same read formats as `file:read()`. By default (`"*l"`), it iterates over lines without the newline character.

```lua
local linesinfile, err = io.open("input.txt", "r")
if linesinfile then
  local count = 0
  for line in linesinfile:lines() do -- Default is '*l' format
    count = count + 1
    print(string.format("Line %d: %s", count, line))
  end
  linesinfile:close() -- Important!
else
  print("Could not open input.txt:", err)
end
```

- **Seeking:** `file:seek([whence [, offset]])`

  - Sets the current file position.
  - `whence` (string): `"set"` (from beginning), `"cur"` (from current position, default), `"end"` (from end).
  - `offset` (number): Byte offset relative to `whence` (default 0).
  - Returns the final file position (from beginning) or `nil` + error.

# Peeking Under the Hood

The `debug` library provides functions for introspection – examining the program's state, particularly the execution stack and variable information. It's primarily intended for building debuggers and diagnostic tools, **not for general application logic.** Using it carelessly can expose internal details and potentially cause issues.

- `debug.getinfo(func | level, [what])`: Returns a table containing information about a function or a stack level. `what` is a string specifying which fields to include (e.g., `"n"` for name, `"S"` for source/line info, `"l"` for current line, `"u"` for number of upvalues, `"f"` for the function itself).
- `debug.getlocal(level | func, localnum)`: Returns the name and value of the local variable with index `localnum` at the given stack `level` or for the given `func`.
- `debug.getupvalue(func, upnum)`: Returns the name and value of the upvalue (a non-local variable accessed by a closure, see Chapter 5) with index `upnum` for the given function `func`.
- `debug.traceback([message [, level]])`: Returns a string containing a stack traceback, similar to what's shown on error. Useful for logging detailed error context (as seen in the `xpcall` example in Chapter 9).
- `debug.debug()`: Enters an interactive debug mode (console-based), allowing inspection of the stack etc. Requires user interaction.
- **Hooks:** `debug.sethook(...)`, `debug.gethook()` allow setting functions to be called on specific events (line execution, function calls/returns). This is the basis for step-by-step debuggers.

Use the `debug` library sparingly and primarily for debugging purposes.

# Table Utilities

While tables are central to Lua (Chapter 6), the core language only provides the constructor `{}` and indexing `[]`/`.`. The `table` library offers essential utility functions for manipulating tables, especially when used as lists/arrays.

- **Sorting:** `table.sort(tbl, [compfunc])`
    - Sorts the elements of table `tbl` **in-place** (modifies the original table).
    - Works on the list part (integer keys 1 through `#tbl`).
    - Uses the standard `<` operator for comparison by default.

- Optionally takes a comparison function `compfunc(a, b)` which should return `true` if a should come before b in the sorted order.

```
local numbers = { 5, 1, 10, 3, -2 }
table.sort(numbers)
print(table.concat(numbers, ", ")) -- Output: -2, 1, 3, 5, 10

local words = { "banana", "Apple", "cherry" }
-- Default sort is case-sensitive
table.sort(words)
print(table.concat(words, ", ")) -- Output: Apple, banana, cherry

-- Sort ignoring case
table.sort(words, function(a, b) return string.lower(a) <
string.lower(b) end)
print(table.concat(words, ", ")) -- Output: Apple, banana, cherry (stays
same)
```

- **Inserting Elements**: `table.insert(tbl, [pos,] value)`
    - Inserts `value` into table `tbl` at integer position `pos`.
    - If pos is omitted, inserts at the end (`#tbl + 1`).
    - Elements at or after pos are shifted up to make space.

```
local letters = { "a", "c", "d" }
table.insert(letters, 2, "b") -- Insert "b" at position 2
print(table.concat(letters, "")) -- Output: abcd
table.insert(letters, "e") -- Insert "e" at the end
print(table.concat(letters, "")) -- Output: abcde
```

- **Removing Elements**: `table.remove(tbl, [pos])`
    - Removes (and returns) the element at integer position pos in table `tbl`.
    - If pos is omitted, removes the *last* element (`#tbl`).
    - Elements after pos are shifted down to fill the gap, keeping the sequence dense (important for # to work correctly).

```
local items = { 10, 20, 30, 40, 50 }
local removedItem = table.remove(items, 3) -- Remove element at index 3
(30)
print("Removed:", removedItem)            -- Output: Removed: 30
print(table.concat(items, ", "))       -- Output: 10, 20, 40, 50

local lastItem = table.remove(items) -- Remove last element (50)
```

```
print("Removed last:", lastItem)        -- Output: Removed last: 50
print(table.concat(items, ", "))        -- Output: 10, 20, 40
```

- **Concatenating Elements:** `table.concat(tbl, [sep,] [i,] [j])`

  - Returns a string formed by concatenating the elements of table `tbl` from index `i` (default 1) to `j` (default `#tbl`).
  - An optional separator string `sep` (default empty string `""`) can be inserted between elements.
  - Elements must be strings or numbers (which are converted to strings).

```
local parts = { "Lua", "is", "fun" }
local sentence = table.concat(parts, " ")
print(sentence) -- Output: Lua is fun

local data = { 1, 2, 3, 4, 5 }
local csv = table.concat(data, ",", 2, 4) -- Elements 2 through 4 with
',' sep
print(csv) -- Output: 2,3,4
```

- **Packing/Unpacking (Variable Arguments):** `table.pack(...)` and `table.unpack(tbl, [i,] [j])`

  - `table.pack(...)`: Takes a variable number of arguments and returns a new table containing all arguments in the integer keys (1, 2, ...), plus an additional field `"n"` holding the total number of arguments. Useful for handling varargs (`...`) passed to a function (similar to `{...}` but adds the `"n"` field).
  - `table.unpack(tbl, [i,] [j])`: Takes a table `tbl` and returns its elements (from index `i` to `j`) as separate return values. Useful for passing table elements as distinct arguments to another function. (In Lua 5.1, this was a global function `unpack`).

```
function printPacked(...)
  local args = table.pack(...)
  print("Number of args:", args.n)
  for i = 1, args.n do
    print(" Arg", i, ":", args[i])
  end
end
printPacked("a", true, 10)
```

```
local myArgs = { "Hello", "World" }
-- Pass elements of myArgs as separate args to print:
print(table.unpack(myArgs)) -- Output: Hello    World
```

# Handling Unicode

Standard Lua string functions (like # and string.sub) operate on **bytes**. This works fine for ASCII, where one byte equals one character. However, for encodings like UTF-8, where characters can span multiple bytes, these functions can give incorrect results if you expect character counts or want to index by character position. Lua 5.3 introduced the utf8 library to correctly handle UTF-8 encoded strings.

- utf8.len(s, [i], [j]): Returns the number of UTF-8 **characters** in string s (optionally between byte positions i and j). Returns nil + position if the sequence is not valid UTF-8.

  ```
  local s_utf8 = "你好世界" -- "Hello World" in Chinese (3 bytes per char)
  print(#s_utf8)         -- Output: 12 (Number of bytes)
  print(utf8.len(s_utf8)) -- Output: 4  (Number of characters)
  ```

- utf8.codes(s): Returns an iterator function (for for loops) that yields the Unicode code point (an integer) for each character in the string s.

  ```
  for codePoint in utf8.codes("Hi Ω") do
    print(codePoint) -- Output: 72 (H), 105 (i), 32 (space), 937 (Omega)
  end
  ```

- utf8.char(...): Takes integer Unicode code points and returns a string encoded in UTF-8.

- utf8.offset(s, n, [i]): Returns the byte position (offset) in string s that corresponds to the n-th character (starting from byte position i).

The utf8 library is essential if your Lua application needs to correctly process text containing characters outside the basic ASCII range.

# Chapter Summary

This chapter provided a tour of Lua's powerful standard libraries, demonstrating that Lua provides much more than just its core syntax. You learned about the math library for calculations, `os` for system interaction (time, files, commands, environment), `io` for detailed file input/output, the `debug` library for introspection (use with care!), the indispensable `table` library for sorting, inserting, removing, and concatenating list-like tables, and finally the `utf8` library (Lua 5.3+) for correctly handling multi-byte UTF-8 characters. Familiarity with these libraries is key to writing effective Lua code quickly, leveraging built-in tools for common programming tasks.

One background process we haven't discussed yet is how Lua manages memory. You create strings, tables, and functions, but you rarely explicitly delete them. How does Lua prevent memory from filling up? The answer lies in automatic memory management through **Garbage Collection**, which we will explore in the next chapter.

# 13

# Automatic Memory Management

Throughout our journey so far, we've been creating variables, strings, tables (lots of tables!), and functions without explicitly worrying about cleaning up afterwards. When a variable goes out of scope (Chapter 5) or a table is no longer referenced (Chapter 6), what happens to the memory it was using? In languages like C or C++, the programmer is responsible for manually allocating memory when needed and, crucially, deallocating (freeing) it when it's no longer required. Forgetting to free memory leads to **memory leaks**, where the program consumes more and more memory over time, eventually crashing or slowing down the system. Freeing memory too early or more than once leads to crashes or corrupted data (dangling pointers, double frees). Manual memory management is powerful but notoriously error-prone.

Lua takes a different approach, freeing you from this burden through **automatic memory management**, commonly known as **Garbage Collection (GC)**. Lua's garbage collector periodically runs in the background, identifies memory chunks that are no longer in use by your program, and reclaims that memory, making it available for future use. This chapter demystifies Lua's GC, explaining the core concepts of how it works, how you can influence it with weak tables and finalizers, and how to interact with the collector if needed.

# Forgetting About Memory (Mostly)

The beauty of automatic garbage collection is that, most of the time, you simply don't have to think about memory allocation or deallocation. You create tables, strings, functions, etc., and Lua figures out when they are no longer needed and cleans them up.

```
function createData()
  local tempTable = { message = "Temporary data" }
  local longString = string.rep("abc", 1000) -- Create a 3000-byte string
  -- Do something with tempTable and longString
  print("Inside function:", tempTable.message)
  -- When the function returns, tempTable and longString become unreachable
  -- (assuming no closures captured them or they weren't returned/stored
elsewhere)
end

createData() -- Function executes
-- After createData() returns, the memory used by the table and the long
-- string inside it becomes eligible for garbage collection.
-- Lua's GC will eventually reclaim it automatically.
```

This simplifies programming significantly and eliminates a whole class of difficult memory management bugs common in other languages.

# How Lua Finds the Garbage

How does Lua *know* which memory is "garbage" and which is still needed? The core principle is **reachability**. An object (like a table, string, function, userdata, or thread) is considered "live" (not garbage) if it can be reached by following a chain of references starting from a set of known "roots."

**What are the Roots?** Roots are the fundamental places where Lua knows live objects must exist:

1. **The Global Table (_G):** Any object directly or indirectly referenced by a global variable is reachable.
2. **The Execution Stack:** Local variables and temporary values currently being used by active functions are reachable.
3. **Upvalues:** Local variables from enclosing functions that are captured by active closures (as discussed in Chapter 5) keep those variables (and the objects they refer to) reachable as long as the closure itself is reachable.

4. **The debug library and C Registry (Advanced):** Other internal structures can also act as roots.

**The Reachability Analogy:** Imagine all your Lua objects are islands floating in an ocean. Some islands have bridges (references) connecting them to other islands. There are a few mainland anchor points (the roots). Any island you can reach by starting at an anchor point and crossing bridges is considered "live". Any island that has no path back to the mainland is considered "garbage" – it's floating free and can be safely removed.

# Lua's Garbage Collection Algorithm

Lua employs a sophisticated **incremental mark-and-sweep** garbage collector. While the exact details have evolved across Lua versions, the fundamental idea remains similar:

1. **Mark Phase:**

   - The collector starts at the roots (globals, stack, etc.).
   - It traverses all reachable objects, following references (like table keys/ values pointing to other objects).
   - Every object it reaches is marked as "live" (conceptually, imagine painting it white). Initially, all objects might be considered "gray" or "black" (not yet processed or confirmed dead).
   - **Incremental:** This marking doesn't usually happen all at once, which could cause a noticeable pause in your program. Instead, the GC does a small amount of marking work, then lets your Lua code run for a bit, then does more marking, and so on. This spreads the GC work over time, reducing pauses.

2. **Sweep Phase:**

   - Once the marking phase believes it has identified all reachable objects, the sweep phase begins.
   - The collector examines *all* objects managed by Lua.
   - Any object that was *not* marked as live during the mark phase is considered garbage.
   - The memory occupied by these unmarked objects is reclaimed and added back to the pool of available memory.
   - **Incremental:** This phase can also run incrementally, sweeping a portion of memory at a time.

3. **Atomic Phase:** While most of the work is incremental, there are typically very short phases where the Lua execution *must* pause briefly for the GC to perform synchronization tasks safely (e.g., starting the marking or finishing the sweep). Lua's GC is designed to keep these pauses as short as possible (often milliseconds or less).

Modern Lua versions (like 5.4) also incorporate techniques like generational garbage collection, which optimize the process by observing that newly created objects often become garbage much faster than older objects. The collector might focus more frequently on scanning younger objects.

**Key Takeaway:** You don't need to memorize the exact algorithm steps. The important concept is that Lua automatically reclaims memory for objects that are no longer reachable from the core parts of your running program.

# Weak References

Normally, if table A contains a reference to table B (e.g., A.field = B), that reference prevents B from being garbage collected as long as A itself is reachable. This is called a **strong reference**.

But what if you want to associate data with an object without preventing that object from being collected if nothing *else* references it? Or what if you want to build a cache where the cached items automatically disappear if they are no longer used elsewhere in the program? This is where **weak tables** come in.

A weak table holds **weak references** to its keys, its values, or both. A weak reference does *not* prevent the referenced object from being garbage collected.

You control the "weakness" of a table via the __mode field in its **metatable** (Chapter 7). The value of __mode should be a string containing:

- "k": Makes the **keys** of the table weak.
- "v": Makes the **values** of the table weak.
- "kv": Makes both **keys and values** weak.

## Weak Values (__mode = "v")

If a table has weak values, a value stored in it will be collected if the *only* reference to that value is from within this weak table. When the value is collected, the key-value pair is removed from the weak table.

**Use Case: Caching** Imagine caching computationally expensive results. You want the cache to hold the result as long as something else is actively using it, but you want the result to disappear from the cache automatically if it becomes unused elsewhere.

```lua
-- cache will hold weak references to the result tables
local cache = {}
setmetatable(cache, { __mode = "v" }) -- Make VALUES weak

function getExpensiveData(id)
  -- Check if data is already cached
  if cache[id] then
    print("Returning cached data for ID:", id)
    return cache[id]
  end

  print("Calculating expensive data for ID:", id)
  local data = { result = string.rep(tostring(id), 5) } -- Simulate calculation
  cache[id] = data -- Store in cache (weakly referenced)
  return data
end

-- --- Usage ---
local data1 = getExpensiveData(1) -- Calculate
print("Data 1:", data1.result)

collectgarbage("collect") -- Force a GC cycle (for demonstration)
print("Cache entry for 1 still exists because 'data1' holds a strong ref.")
print("Cache[1] =", cache[1])

local data2 = getExpensiveData(2) -- Calculate
print("Data 2:", data2.result)

data1 = nil -- Remove the *only* strong reference to the data for ID 1

print("\nRemoved strong reference to data1.")
collectgarbage("collect") -- Force another GC cycle

print("Cache entry for 1 should now be gone:")
print("Cache[1] =", cache[1]) -- Output: Cache[1] = nil (Value was collected)
print("Cache entry for 2 still exists because 'data2' holds a strong ref.")
print("Cache[2] =", cache[2]) -- Output: Cache[2] = table: 0x......
```

# Weak Keys (`__mode = "k"`)

If a table has weak keys, a key-value pair will be removed if the *only* reference to the **key object** is from within this weak table. This is less common than weak values but useful for associating data with objects you don't "own".

**Use Case: Object Metadata** Suppose you have objects (maybe userdata from C, or tables representing something external) and you want to attach some extra Lua-side information to them without preventing the original objects from being collected if they go out of scope.

```lua
local metadata = {}
setmetatable(metadata, { __mode = "k" }) -- Make KEYS weak

function createObject(name)
  local obj = { name = name } -- Simulate an object
  metadata[obj] = { last_accessed = os.time() } -- Associate metadata
  return obj
end

local objA = createObject("Object A")
local objB = createObject("Object B")

print("Metadata for objA:", metadata[objA].last_accessed)
print("Metadata for objB:", metadata[objB].last_accessed)

objA = nil -- Remove the only strong reference to the key object 'objA'

print("\nRemoved strong reference to objA.")
collectgarbage("collect") -- Force GC

print("Metadata for objA should be gone:")
-- Accessing metadata[objA] might now give nil or error if objA was truly
collected
-- We can check by iterating (pairs might or might not show it immediately after
GC)
local foundA = false
for k, v in pairs(metadata) do
    if k == objA then foundA = true end -- This comparison might fail if objA is
gone
    -- A better check might be comparing the name if available inside metadata
value
    print(" Remaining key name:", k.name) -- Accessing k assumes key still valid
end
if not foundA then
    print(" Metadata for Object A seems collected (key is gone).")
```

```
    end
    print("Metadata for objB:", metadata[objB].last_accessed) -- Still exists
```

*(Note: Demonstrating weak key collection perfectly is tricky without userdata, as comparing col-
lected table keys can be ambiguous. The principle holds: if the key object is gone, the entry is
removed).*

# Running Code Before Cleanup

What if an object managed by Lua (like userdata representing a C file handle, or a
table managing network resources) needs to perform some cleanup action just before
it's garbage collected? Lua provides the __gc metamethod for this purpose.

If a table or userdata has a metatable with a __gc field, and an object of that type is
about to be collected (because it became unreachable), Lua will:

1.  Mark the object as "finalized".
2.  Place the object in a special list of objects awaiting finalization.
3.  Later (usually during a subsequent GC cycle), Lua will fetch the __gc meta-
    method associated with the object and call it, passing the object itself as the
    sole argument.
4.  Only after the __gc method has been called (and potentially in a later cycle
    still) will the object's memory actually be reclaimed.

```
local FileWrapperMeta = {}
FileWrapperMeta.__index = FileWrapperMeta -- Allow method calls

function FileWrapperMeta:__gc()
  print("GC triggered for FileWrapper:", self.filename)
  if self.handle and not self.closed then
    print("  Closing file handle for:", self.filename)
    -- In a real scenario with userdata, this would call the C close function
    self.closed = true
    -- self.handle:close() -- If handle were a real Lua file object
  end
end

function createWrapper(filename)
  print("Creating wrapper for:", filename)
  local wrapper = {
    filename = filename,
    handle = io.open(filename, "w"), -- Simulate getting a resource handle
    closed = false
```

```
    }
    if not wrapper.handle then return nil end -- Handle open error
    return setmetatable(wrapper, FileWrapperMeta)
end

-- Create a wrapper, write to it, then lose the reference
local fw = createWrapper("temp_gc_file.txt")
if fw then
    fw.handle:write("Data to be finalized.\n")
    -- Intentionally DON'T close fw.handle here
end

fw = nil -- Lose the only strong reference to the wrapper table

print("\nLost reference to FileWrapper. Forcing GC...")
collectgarbage("collect") -- GC identifies fw as garbage, marks for finalization
print("GC cycle 1 finished. Finalizer might not have run yet.")
collectgarbage("collect") -- Next GC cycle likely runs the pending finalizers
print("GC cycle 2 finished.")

-- Clean up the temp file created by the example
os.remove("temp_gc_file.txt")
```

**Output (Order of GC messages might vary slightly):**

```
Creating wrapper for: temp_gc_file.txt

Lost reference to FileWrapper. Forcing GC...
GC cycle 1 finished. Finalizer might not have run yet.
GC triggered for FileWrapper: temp_gc_file.txt
  Closing file handle for: temp_gc_file.txt
GC cycle 2 finished.
```

**Important Considerations for __gc:**

- **Primary Use:** Essential for releasing external resources (C memory, file handles, sockets, database connections, locks) managed by userdata. Less commonly needed for pure Lua tables unless they manage external state indirectly.
- **No Guaranteed Order:** If multiple objects with finalizers become unreachable in the same cycle, the order in which their __gc methods are called is not specified.
- **Resurrection:** Avoid creating new strong references to the object *inside* its __gc method. Doing so can "resurrect" the object, preventing its memory from

142

being reclaimed in that cycle (though it might be collected later if the new reference is also dropped).

- **Errors:** Errors occurring inside a `__gc` method are typically caught and reported by Lua (often to `stderr`), but they don't usually stop the finalization of other objects or the GC process itself.

# Interacting with the Garbage Collector

While Lua's GC is automatic, the `collectgarbage()` function provides a way to interact with it directly or tune its behavior. You generally **do not need** to call this in typical applications. Lua's adaptive GC usually does a good job on its own.

Common opt strings for `collectgarbage(opt, [arg])`:

- `"collect"`: Performs a *full* garbage collection cycle (mark and sweep). Use sparingly, perhaps only during idle times or for debugging, as it can cause a noticeable pause.
- `"stop"`: Stops the automatic running of the garbage collector. **Use with extreme caution!** If you stop the GC and your program continues allocating memory, it will eventually run out of memory and crash.
- `"restart"`: Restarts the automatic garbage collector if it was previously stopped.
- `"count"`: Returns the total memory currently in use by Lua (in kilobytes, as a floating-point number). Useful for monitoring memory usage.
- `"step"`: Performs a single incremental GC step. The optional `arg` number controls how much work is done (in an internal unit). Returns `true` if the step completed a full GC cycle. Can be used to perform GC work explicitly during application idle periods instead of relying solely on the automatic triggering.
- `"isrunning"`: (Lua 5.1+) Returns `true` if the automatic collector is running (hasn't been stopped).
- `"setpause"`: Sets the collector's "pause" value (as a percentage, `arg`). A value of 200 (the default) means the collector waits until total memory doubles before starting a new cycle after finishing one. Lower values make the GC run more aggressively (more often); higher values make it run less often.
- `"setstepmul"`: Sets the collector's "step multiplier" (as a percentage, `arg`). This controls how much work the GC does in each incremental step relative to the rate of memory allocation. Higher values make the GC more aggressive during a cycle.

- **"incremental"** / **"generational"**: (Lua 5.4+) Switches between GC modes. Generational is generally preferred and often the default.

**When might you use** `collectgarbage`?

- **Debugging**: Forcing `"collect"` after releasing references to check if memory is behaving as expected, or using `"count"` to monitor memory usage.
- **Real-time Systems**: In systems with strict timing requirements, you might `"stop"` the GC during critical sections and perform explicit `"step"`s or a full `"collect"` during safe idle periods (this requires careful management).
- **Performance Tuning**: Only after profiling reveals that the default GC behavior is causing significant performance issues, you *might* experiment *carefully* with `"setpause"` and `"setstepmul"`.

For most applications, leave the GC settings alone and let Lua manage things automatically.

# Performance Considerations & Good Practices

- **Minimize Garbage**: While GC is automatic, it's not free. Creating and discarding large numbers of objects (especially tables) very rapidly in tight loops *can* put pressure on the GC and consume CPU time. If performance is critical in such a loop, consider reusing tables or objects instead of creating new ones on every iteration.
- **Weak Tables for Caches**: Use weak tables (`__mode = "v"`) appropriately for caches to allow cached items to be collected automatically when no longer strongly referenced elsewhere.
- **`__gc` for External Resources**: Use finalizers primarily for releasing non-Lua resources tied to userdata.
- **Profile First**: Don't guess about performance bottlenecks. Use profiling tools (even simple `os.clock()` timings) to identify where your program spends its time *before* considering GC tuning or complex object pooling optimizations. Often, the bottleneck lies in your algorithm or other parts of the code, not the GC itself.

# Chapter Summary

This chapter lifted the veil on Lua's automatic memory management. You learned that Lua uses a garbage collector (typically an incremental mark-and-sweep variant) to reclaim memory from objects that are no longer reachable from program roots (globals, stack, etc.). We explored how weak tables (using the `__mode` metatable field with "k", "v", or "kv") allow references that *don't* prevent garbage collection, useful for caches and object metadata. You discovered the `__gc` metamethod (finalizer), which allows code (usually for cleanup of external resources) to run just before an object's memory is reclaimed. Finally, we looked at the `collectgarbage()` function for interacting with and tuning the GC, emphasizing that manual control is rarely needed. Lua's GC frees you from manual memory management, letting you focus on your application's logic, but understanding its principles helps write more efficient and robust code.

So far, we've focused entirely on programming *within* Lua. One of Lua's original design goals and greatest strengths, however, is its ability to interact seamlessly with code written in other languages, particularly C. In the next chapter, we'll explore the Lua C API, the bridge that allows you to extend Lua with C functions and embed the Lua interpreter within your C/C++ applications.

# 14

# Extending Lua

Lua, as we've seen, is a powerful yet simple language. Its strengths lie in its flexibility, speed (for a scripting language), and small footprint. However, sometimes you need more raw performance for computationally intensive tasks, access to specific operating system features, or the ability to use vast existing libraries written in lower-level languages like C. Furthermore, one of Lua's most significant design goals was to be **embeddable** – to serve as a scripting engine *inside* a larger application written in C or C++. This chapter introduces the **Lua C API**, the Application Programming Interface that acts as the bridge between the Lua world and the C world, enabling these powerful interactions.

## Why Bridge Lua and C?

There are several compelling reasons to integrate Lua and C:

1. **Performance:** While Lua is fast, computationally demanding algorithms (like complex physics simulations, heavy data processing, or cryptographic operations) often run significantly faster when implemented in compiled C code. You can write the bulk of your application in Lua for flexibility and use C for the critical performance bottlenecks.

2. **Access to Existing C Libraries:** The world is full of mature, highly optimized C libraries for graphics, networking, databases, scientific computing, hardware

interaction, and more. The C API allows your Lua code to leverage these libraries without rewriting them in Lua.

3. **System/Hardware Access:** C provides direct access to low-level operating system features and hardware interactions that might not be exposed through Lua's standard os library.

4. **Embedding Lua:** Many applications benefit from an integrated scripting language to allow users or developers to customize behavior, automate tasks, or define configurations. Lua's small size and clean API make it an excellent choice for embedding within a larger C or C++ application. The C application can expose specific functionality to the Lua environment and run Lua scripts provided by the user.

# The Lua C API

The Lua C API is a set of C functions provided by the Lua library (`liblua.a` or `lua.dll`/`liblua.so`) that allow C code to interact with a running Lua **state**.

- **The Lua State** (`lua_State*`): Every interaction with Lua from C happens through a pointer to a `lua_State`. This opaque structure represents an independent Lua environment (containing its own globals, stack, loaded modules, etc.). You can have multiple Lua states running concurrently within a single C application. You create a state using `luaL_newstate()` (usually from `lauxlib.h`) and close it using `lua_close()`.

- **Header Files**: To use the API, your C code needs to include the Lua header files:
    - `lua.h`: Defines the basic API functions (`lua_push*`, `lua_to*`, `lua_pcall`, etc.).
    - `lauxlib.h`: Defines higher-level auxiliary functions built upon the basic API, making common tasks easier (e.g., `luaL_newstate`, `luaL_loadfile`, `luaL_checkstring`). These functions typically start with `luaL_`.
    - `lualib.h`: Provides functions to open the standard Lua libraries (`luaL_openlibs`).

Crucially, the C API does **not** allow direct access to Lua object internals (like the fields of a C struct representing a Lua table). All interactions happen indirectly through a controlled mechanism: the virtual stack.

# The Core Concept

Instead of directly manipulating Lua data structures, C code communicates with a specific `lua_State` using a **virtual stack** managed by Lua. Think of it like a shared workspace or a stack of plates where C and Lua can leave values for each other.

- **C Pushes:** When C wants to pass a value (number, string, table) *to* Lua, it **pushes** that value onto the top of the stack associated with the `lua_State`.
- **C Gets:** When C wants to get a value *from* Lua (e.g., a result returned by a Lua function, or a global variable), it uses API functions that read values from specific positions on the stack.
- **Lua Interaction:** When C calls a Lua function, Lua takes its arguments from the stack. When a Lua function returns values, it pushes them onto the stack. When a C function called *by* Lua returns, it pushes its results onto the stack.

**Stack Indexing:** You refer to positions on the stack using integer indices:

- **Positive Indices:** 1 refers to the bottom element (the first element pushed), 2 to the second, and so on.
- **Negative Indices:** -1 refers to the top element (the most recently pushed), -2 to the element just below the top, and so on.

Using negative indices is often more convenient because you don't need to know exactly how many items are currently on the stack; -1 always refers to the top.

The C API provides functions to push data onto the stack, query data at specific indices, convert data at indices to C types, call functions, and manipulate the stack itself (e.g., removing elements, inserting elements).

# Pushing Values onto the Stack (C -> Lua)

These functions take a `lua_State*` (usually named L by convention) and the C value to push. They place the corresponding Lua value on the top of the stack (index -1).

- `void lua_pushnil(lua_State *L);` - Pushes the Lua value `nil`.
- `void lua_pushboolean(lua_State *L, int b);` - Pushes `true` if b is non-zero, `false` otherwise.
- `void lua_pushnumber(lua_State *L, lua_Number n);` - Pushes a floating-point number. (`lua_Number` is typically `double`).
- `void lua_pushinteger(lua_State *L, lua_Integer n);` - Pushes an integer. (`lua_Integer` is typically `ptrdiff_t` or `long long`).

- `const char *lua_pushstring(lua_State *L, const char *s);` - Pushes a null-terminated C string. Lua makes its own internal copy. Returns a pointer to Lua's internal copy.
- `const char *lua_pushlstring(lua_State *L, const char *s, size_t len);` - Pushes a C string with an explicit length (can contain embedded nulls). Lua makes its own internal copy. Returns a pointer to Lua's internal copy.
- `void lua_pushcfunction(lua_State *L, lua_CFunction f);` - Pushes a C function (see later). `lua_CFunction` is a function pointer type: `typedef int (*lua_CFunction) (lua_State *L);`.
- `void lua_pushcclosure(lua_State *L, lua_CFunction f, int nup);` - Pushes a C closure (a C function associated with nup upvalues, which are popped from the stack).
- `void lua_createtable(lua_State *L, int narr, int nrec);` - Creates a new empty table and pushes it onto the stack. `narr` and `nrec` are hints about array and record sizes for pre-allocation.
- `void lua_pushvalue(lua_State *L, int index);` - Pushes a *copy* of the element at the given `index` onto the top of the stack.

```
/* Conceptual C Snippet */
#include "lua.h"
#include "lauxlib.h"

// Assume 'L' is a valid lua_State*

lua_pushstring(L, "Hello from C!"); // Stack: ["Hello from C!"]
lua_pushinteger(L, 123);            // Stack: ["Hello from C!", 123]
lua_pushboolean(L, 1);              // Stack: ["Hello from C!", 123, true]
lua_pushvalue(L, 1);                // Stack: ["Hello from C!", 123, true, "Hello
from C!"]
                                    //        (index 1 copied to top)
```

# Getting Values from the Stack (Lua -> C)

These functions retrieve values from a given stack `index`. **It's crucial to check the type of the value on the stack before trying to convert it!**

- **Type Checking:**
    - `int lua_isnumber(lua_State *L, int index);` (True for integers and floats)

- `int lua_isstring(lua_State *L, int index);` (True for strings and numbers - numbers are convertible)
- `int lua_isboolean(lua_State *L, int index);`
- `int lua_istable(lua_State *L, int index);`
- `int lua_isfunction(lua_State *L, int index);` (True for Lua and C functions)
- `int lua_isnil(lua_State *L, int index);`
- `int lua_type(lua_State *L, int index);` Returns a type code constant (e.g., `LUA_TSTRING`, `LUA_TNUMBER`). `lua_typename(L, type_code)` gives the string name.

- **Retrieving Values:** These functions attempt to convert the value at `index` to the desired C type. If the value is not convertible, they might return 0, `NULL`, or an undefined value (depending on the function). **Always check the type first using `lua_is*` or use the `luaL_check*` auxiliary functions.**

  - `int lua_toboolean(lua_State *L, int index);` (Returns 0 for `false` and `nil`, 1 otherwise - Lua's truthiness).
  - `lua_Number lua_tonumber(lua_State *L, int index);` (Use `lua_isnumber` first).
  - `lua_Integer lua_tointeger(lua_State *L, int index);` (Use `lua_isinteger` or `lua_isnumber` first).
  - `const char *lua_tolstring(lua_State *L, int index, size_t *len);` Returns a pointer to an internal string representation (use `len` if needed for length). **Important:** The returned pointer is valid only as long as the string value remains on the stack. Do **not** store this pointer long-term; copy the string data if needed. If `len` is `NULL`, it's not populated. `lua_tostring` is a macro equivalent to calling `lua_tolstring` with `len = NULL`.
  - `lua_CFunction lua_tocfunction(lua_State *L, int index);`

- `luaL_check*` **Auxiliary Functions (Recommended):** These functions from `lauxlib.h` combine the type check and retrieval. If the type check fails, they automatically raise a standard Lua error, which is often the desired behavior when writing C functions called *by* Lua.

  - `lua_Number luaL_checknumber(lua_State *L, int index);`
  - `lua_Integer luaL_checkinteger(lua_State *L, int index);`
  - `const char *luaL_checklstring(lua_State *L, int index, size_t *len);`

- void luaL_checktype(lua_State *L, int index, int type_code);
  (Checks for a specific LUA_T* type).
- **Table Manipulation:**

  - int lua_gettable(lua_State *L, int index); Pops a key from the stack, looks it up in the table at index, and pushes the result. Returns the type of the pushed value.
  - int lua_getfield(lua_State *L, int index, const char *key); Pushes table[key] onto the stack, where table is at index. Returns the type of the pushed value. (Convenience).
  - void lua_settable(lua_State *L, int index); Pops a value, then a key from the stack, and performs table[key] = value, where table is at index.
  - void lua_setfield(lua_State *L, int index, const char *key); Pops a value from the stack and performs table[key] = value, where table is at index. (Convenience).

```c
/* Conceptual C Snippet */
#include "lua.h"
#include "lauxlib.h"

// Assume L is valid and stack holds: ["Hello", 123, true, {k="v"}]

// Using basic API (careful checking needed)
if (lua_isstring(L, 1)) {
    size_t len;
    const char *str = lua_tolstring(L, 1, &len);
    printf("Index 1 (string): %s (len %zu)\n", str, len);
}
if (lua_isinteger(L, 2)) {
    lua_Integer i = lua_tointeger(L, 2);
    printf("Index 2 (integer): %lld\n", (long long)i);
}

// Using auxiliary API (safer when called from Lua)
// const char* str_checked = luaL_checkstring(L, 1);
// lua_Integer int_checked = luaL_checkinteger(L, 2);

// Get table field
lua_getfield(L, 4, "k"); // Pushes the value of table at index 4, key "k"
                         // Stack: ["Hello", 123, true, {k="v"}, "v"]
if (lua_isstring(L, -1)) { // Check the newly pushed value at the top
    printf("Table field 'k': %s\n", lua_tostring(L, -1));
}
```

```
lua_pop(L, 1); // Remove the retrieved value from the stack
              // Stack: ["Hello", 123, true, {k="v"}]
```

# Calling Lua Functions from C

To execute a Lua function from your C code:

1. **Push the Function:** Get the Lua function onto the stack (e.g., using `lua_getglobal(L, "myLuaFunction")` to get a global function).

2. **Push Arguments:** Push all the arguments the Lua function expects onto the stack in order.

3. **Call** `lua_pcall`**:** Use `int lua_pcall(lua_State *L, int nargs, int nresults, int msgh)`;

    - `nargs`: The number of arguments you pushed onto the stack.
    - `nresults`: The number of return values you expect Lua to push onto the stack. Use `LUA_MULTRET` if the function can return a variable number of results.
    - `msgh`: Stack index of an *error handler function* (or 0 for no handler). If an error occurs during the Lua function execution, Lua calls this handler *before* unwinding the stack. The handler can process the error (e.g., add a traceback). `lua_pcall` then returns an error code. If `msgh` is 0, the error object is left on the stack on failure.
    - **Return Code:** `lua_pcall` returns `LUA_OK` (0) on success, or an error code (e.g., `LUA_ERRRUN`, `LUA_ERRMEM`) on failure.

4. **Retrieve Results:** If `lua_pcall` returned `LUA_OK`, the expected number of results (`nresults`) will be on the top of the stack. Retrieve them using `lua_to*` functions.

5. **Clean Up:** The function and arguments are automatically removed from the stack by `lua_pcall`. You need to pop the results (or the error message) after you are done with them.

```c
/* Conceptual C Snippet */
int callLuaFunction(lua_State *L, const char* funcName, int arg1, int arg2) {
    int result = 0;
    int error = 0;

    // 1. Push the function
    lua_getglobal(L, funcName);
    if (!lua_isfunction(L, -1)) {
```

```
        fprintf(stderr, "Error: '%s' is not a function\n", funcName);
        lua_pop(L, 1); // remove non-function value
        return -1; // Indicate error
    }

    // 2. Push arguments
    lua_pushinteger(L, arg1);
    lua_pushinteger(L, arg2);

    // 3. Call lua_pcall (2 arguments, expecting 1 result, no error handler)
    error = lua_pcall(L, 2, 1, 0);

    if (error == LUA_OK) {
        // 4. Retrieve result (check type first!)
        if (lua_isinteger(L, -1)) {
            result = (int)lua_tointeger(L, -1);
        } else {
            fprintf(stderr, "Error: Lua function did not return an integer\n");
            result = -1; // Indicate error
        }
        lua_pop(L, 1); // Pop the result
    } else {
        // Error occurred during pcall
        const char *errorMsg = lua_tostring(L, -1); // Get error message
        fprintf(stderr, "Error running Lua function '%s': %s\n", funcName,
errorMsg);
        lua_pop(L, 1); // Pop the error message
        result = -1; // Indicate error
    }

    return result;
}
```

# Calling C Functions from Lua

This is how you extend Lua's capabilities.

1. **Write the C Function:** It must have the signature int
   `my_c_function(lua_State *L);`

   - Arguments passed from Lua will be on the stack (index 1, 2, ...).
   - Use `lua_to*` or `luaL_check*` to retrieve arguments.
   - Perform the desired C logic.
   - Push any return values onto the stack using `lua_push*`.

- Return an integer indicating the *number* of values you pushed onto the stack as results.

```
/* C function callable from Lua */
static int c_add(lua_State *L) {
    // 1. Get arguments (using check functions for safety)
    lua_Integer a = luaL_checkinteger(L, 1); // Arg at index 1
    lua_Integer b = luaL_checkinteger(L, 2); // Arg at index 2

    // 2. Perform C logic
    lua_Integer sum = a + b;

    // 3. Push the result
    lua_pushinteger(L, sum);

    // 4. Return the number of results pushed (1 in this case)
    return 1;
}
```

2. **Register the C Function:** Make the C function known to Lua. You can:

   - Push it onto the stack and assign it to a global variable:

     ```
     lua_pushcfunction(L, c_add);
     lua_setglobal(L, "c_add_function"); // Lua can now call
     c_add_function(10, 20)
     ```

   - Add it to a table (the preferred way for creating libraries/modules): See next section.

# Writing C Libraries (Modules) for Lua

The standard way to package multiple related C functions for use in Lua is to create a shared library (like .so on Linux, .dll on Windows) that Lua can load using `require`.

1. **Define Functions:** Write your C functions using the `int func(lua_State *L)` signature.
2. **Create Registration Array:** Define a static array of `luaL_Reg` structs. Each struct maps a name (string, how it will be called from Lua) to the C function pointer. The array must end with a {NULL, NULL} entry.

   ```
   static const struct luaL_Reg mylibrary_funcs[] = {
       {"add", c_add}, // Lua name "add" maps to C function c_add
   ```

```
        // {"subtract", c_subtract}, // Add more functions here...
        {NULL, NULL} /* Sentinel */
    };
```

3. **Write the** `luaopen_` **Function:** Create a special function named
   `luaopen_mylibraryname` (where `mylibraryname` matches the name Lua will
   use in `require`). This function is called automatically by `require` when loading the C library. Its job is to create the module table and register the functions.

   ```
   #include "lua.h"
   #include "lauxlib.h"

   // Include definitions for c_add etc.

   /* Registration array from step 2 */
   static const struct luaL_Reg myclibrary_funcs[] = { ... };

   /* Library opening function */
   LUALIB_API int luaopen_myclibrary(lua_State *L) {
       luaL_newlib(L, myclibrary_funcs); // Creates table, registers
   functions
       return 1; // Return the module table pushed by luaL_newlib
   }
   ```

   `luaL_newlib` (from `lauxlib.h`) conveniently creates a new table, iterates
   through the `luaL_Reg` array, and registers each C function into the table using
   the specified Lua names. It leaves the newly created module table on the stack.

4. **Compile as Shared Library:** Compile your C code into a shared library (e.g.,
   `myclibrary.so` or `myclibrary.dll`). Ensure you link against the Lua library
   (`liblua.a` or equivalent). The exact compiler flags depend on your OS and
   compiler (e.g., `-shared -fPIC` with GCC on Linux).

5. **Use in Lua:** Place the compiled library file (`myclibrary.so/.dll`) somewhere
   Lua's C path (`package.cpath`) can find it (often the current directory works).
   Then use `require` in Lua:

   ```
   -- my_script.lua
   local mylib = require("myclibrary") -- Loads .so/.dll, calls
   luaopen_myclibrary

   local result = mylib.add(15, 7) -- Call the C function via the module
   table
   ```

```
print("Result from C:", result) -- Output: Result from C: 22
```

# Error Handling in the C API

- **Calling Lua:** Always use `lua_pcall` instead of `lua_call` (which doesn't handle errors) when calling Lua functions from C, unless you are certain the Lua code cannot fail. Check the return code of `lua_pcall`.
- **Raising Errors from C:** Inside a C function called *by* Lua, use `lua_error(L)` or the more convenient `luaL_error(L, formatstring, ...)` to stop execution and propagate an error back to Lua. `luaL_error` takes a printf-style format string and arguments. These errors can then be caught in Lua using `pcall`.
- **Checking API Returns:** Some basic API functions might return error codes or `NULL` (though many simply manipulate the stack). Check the documentation for functions you use. The `luaL_check*` functions help by automatically raising errors on type mismatches.

# Memory Management Notes

- **Lua Objects:** As discussed in Chapter 13, Lua's garbage collector manages the memory for objects *created by Lua* (strings pushed with `lua_pushstring`, tables from `lua_createtable`, etc.). You don't free these directly from C.
- `lua_tolstring` **Pointer:** Remember the pointer returned by `lua_tolstring` is temporary. Copy the string contents if you need them after the value leaves the stack.
- **Userdata:** What if C needs to allocate memory (e.g., for a large C struct) that Lua should manage? This is done using **userdata**.
  - `void *lua_newuserdatauv(lua_State *L, size_t size, int nuvalue);` Allocates `size` bytes of memory managed by Lua's GC, associates `nuvalue` Lua values (uservalues) with it, and pushes the userdata object onto the stack. You get a raw `void*` pointer to the memory block.
  - You can associate a metatable with userdata, just like tables. This is crucial for defining operations (using metamethods like `__add`, `__index`) and especially for defining a `__gc` metamethod (a finalizer) to release any associated C resources when Lua garbage collects the userdata.

- Userdata allows C data to be treated almost like a first-class Lua object. This is a more advanced topic but fundamental to integrating complex C structures with Lua.

# Chapter Summary

This chapter provided a crucial introduction to the Lua C API, the interface enabling powerful two-way communication between Lua and C. You learned about the central role of the `lua_State` and the virtual stack used for data exchange. We covered pushing C values onto the stack (`lua_push*`) and retrieving Lua values from the stack (`lua_to*`, `luaL_check*`). You saw the procedures for calling Lua functions from C using `lua_pcall` and, conversely, how to write and register C functions (`int func(lua_State *L)`) to be callable *from* Lua. We explored the standard method for creating C libraries (modules) using `luaL_Reg` and `luaopen_` functions, loadable via `require`. We also briefly touched upon error handling across the boundary and the concept of userdata for integrating C-allocated data with Lua's garbage collector.

Understanding the C API unlocks Lua's potential for high performance and integration with existing systems. While we focused on C, similar principles apply when interacting with other languages that have C bindings (like C++).

Now that we've seen how to extend Lua with C, let's return to pure Lua and explore how its flexible table and metatable system can be used to implement patterns from a different programming paradigm: object-oriented programming.

# 15

# Simulating Objects

Throughout this book, we've explored Lua's core features: its versatile tables (Chapter 6), first-class functions (Chapter 5), and the powerful customization layer provided by metatables (Chapter 7). While Lua doesn't include explicit keywords like `class`, `private`, or `interface` found in traditional object-oriented programming (OOP) languages such as Java, C++, or Python, its fundamental building blocks are perfectly suited for implementing OOP concepts and patterns in a flexible and elegant way. This chapter demonstrates how you can leverage tables and metatables to simulate classes, objects, methods, inheritance, and encapsulation in Lua, adopting the object-oriented style when it benefits your program's structure and design.

## Lua's Flexible Approach to OOP

Object-oriented programming revolves around the idea of "objects" – self-contained units that bundle together data (attributes or properties) and behavior (methods or functions that operate on that data). Lua achieves this not through rigid syntax but through clever use of its existing features:

- **Tables as Objects:** An individual object's state (its data) is naturally represented by a Lua table, where keys hold attribute names and values hold the corresponding data.

- **Tables as Classes/Prototypes:** The shared behavior (methods) for a group of similar objects can be stored in another table, often referred to as a "class" or, perhaps more accurately in Lua's case, a "prototype" table.
- **Metatables as the Glue:** The magic connection between an object (instance table) and its shared behavior (class/prototype table) is typically established using the `__index` metamethod. This allows an object to delegate lookups for missing fields (especially methods) to its designated prototype.

This approach offers considerable flexibility. You can choose patterns that closely mimic classical inheritance or lean more towards prototype-based styles where objects inherit directly from other objects. The key is understanding how to combine tables and metatables effectively.

# Representing Objects and Classes

Let's start with the basics: representing the data and the shared behavior.

## Objects as Tables

An object instance simply needs to hold its own unique data. A plain table is perfect for this.

```lua
-- Represents a specific car object
local myCar = {
  make = "Lua Motors",
  model = "Scriptster",
  color = "blue",
  speed = 0
}

-- Represents another car object
local neighborsCar = {
  make = "TableTech",
  model = "Array GT",
  color = "red",
  speed = 0
}

print(myCar.make)        -- Output: Lua Motors
print(neighborsCar.color) -- Output: red
```

These tables hold the *state* specific to each car. But how do we make them *do* something, like accelerate?

## Classes (or Prototypes) as Tables

We can define a separate table to hold the functions (methods) that all cars should share. Let's call this our `Vehicle` prototype.

```lua
-- Represents the shared behavior for vehicles
local Vehicle = {}

-- We'll add methods to this table soon...
-- function Vehicle:accelerate(amount) ... end
-- function Vehicle:brake(amount) ... end

-- We might also include default values here if desired
Vehicle.defaultTopSpeed = 120
```

This `Vehicle` table holds the *behavior* or serves as a template. Now, how do we connect `myCar` to `Vehicle` so `myCar` can use `Vehicle`'s methods? First, we need to understand how methods work with the `self` concept.

# Methods and the Colon Operator (:)

In OOP, methods typically operate on the specific object they were called on. For instance, when you call `myCar:accelerate()`, the `accelerate` function needs to know *which* car object (`myCar`) to modify. Lua handles this association elegantly using the colon (:) operator, which provides syntactic sugar for passing the object instance implicitly.

## Defining Methods

When you define a function within your class/prototype table using the colon notation, Lua automatically adds a hidden first parameter named `self`.

```lua
local Vehicle = {}

-- Define the 'accelerate' method using ':'
function Vehicle:accelerate(amount)
  -- 'self' automatically refers to the object the method is called on
  -- (e.g., myCar when calling myCar:accelerate())
  print("Accelerating...")
  self.speed = self.speed + amount
  print("Current speed:", self.speed)
end
```

160

```
-- Define the 'brake' method
function Vehicle:brake(amount)
  print("Braking...")
  self.speed = self.speed - amount
  if self.speed < 0 then self.speed = 0 end -- Can't have negative speed
  print("Current speed:", self.speed)
end
```

Writing function `Vehicle:accelerate(amount)` is exactly equivalent to writing `Vehicle.accelerate = function(self, amount)`. The colon just saves you from typing `self` explicitly in the parameter list.

## Calling Methods

When you *call* a function using the colon notation (`object:methodName(args...)`), Lua automatically inserts the `object` itself as the very first argument passed to the function.

```
-- Assume myCar is properly linked to Vehicle (we'll show how next)
-- myCar:accelerate(30)

-- This call is syntactic sugar for:
-- Vehicle.accelerate(myCar, 30)
```

The colon operator handles the passing of the object (`myCar`) as the `self` parameter to the method (`Vehicle.accelerate`). This makes method calls clean and object-focused.

# Achieving Inheritance with __index

Now, let's connect the instance (`myCar`) with the prototype (`Vehicle`) so that when we call `myCar:accelerate()`, Lua finds the `accelerate` function in the `Vehicle` table. We use the `__index` metamethod, as introduced in Chapter 7.

The most common pattern is to set the `__index` field of an instance's metatable to point directly to the prototype table.

```
local Vehicle = {} -- Our prototype / class table

function Vehicle:accelerate(amount)
```

```lua
    self.speed = (self.speed or 0) + amount -- Handle potential nil speed
    print("Accelerating to:", self.speed)
end

function Vehicle:brake(amount)
    self.speed = (self.speed or 0) - amount
    if self.speed < 0 then self.speed = 0 end
    print("Braking to:", self.speed)
end

-- Create an instance table
local myCar = { make = "Lua Motors", speed = 0 }

-- Create the metatable for the instance
local mt = {
    __index = Vehicle -- If a key is not found in myCar, look in Vehicle
}

-- Attach the metatable to the instance
setmetatable(myCar, mt)

-- Now, let's try calling a method:
myCar:accelerate(50) -- Lua looks for 'accelerate' in myCar -> not found.
                     -- Checks metatable.__index -> finds Vehicle.
                     -- Looks for 'accelerate' in Vehicle -> found!
                     -- Calls Vehicle.accelerate(myCar, 50)

myCar:brake(20)      -- Works similarly.

print(myCar.speed)   -- Accesses data directly from myCar.
```

## Output:

```
Accelerating to: 50
Braking to: 30
30
```

This `__index = PrototypeTable` setup is the core mechanism for simulating classes and single inheritance in Lua. The instance holds its own data, and method lookups are delegated to the shared prototype table.

# Constructor Functions

Manually creating an instance table and setting its metatable every time is tedious and error-prone. The standard practice is to define a **constructor function**, conventionally named new, within the prototype/class table. This function handles the creation and setup of new instances.

```lua
local Vehicle = {}
Vehicle.__index = Vehicle -- Make methods callable on the class table itself
*and*
                          -- simplify setting __index in the constructor.

-- Constructor function
function Vehicle:new(make, model, color)
  print("Creating new vehicle:", make, model)
  -- 1. Create an empty instance table
  local instance = {}

  -- Initialize instance-specific data
  instance.make = make or "Unknown Make"
  instance.model = model or "Unknown Model"
  instance.color = color or "black"
  instance.speed = 0

  -- 2. Set its metatable to enable method lookup (__index = Vehicle)
  setmetatable(instance, self) -- 'self' here refers to the Vehicle table itself
                               -- because we called Vehicle:new()

  -- 3. Return the new instance
  return instance
end

-- Methods (defined as before)
function Vehicle:accelerate(amount)
  self.speed = (self.speed or 0) + amount
  print(self.make .. " accelerating to:", self.speed)
end

function Vehicle:brake(amount)
  self.speed = (self.speed or 0) - amount
  if self.speed < 0 then self.speed = 0 end
  print(self.make .. " braking to:", self.speed)
end

-- --- Usage ---
local car1 = Vehicle:new("Lua Motors", "Scriptster", "blue")
```

```
local car2 = Vehicle:new("TableTech", "Array GT", "red")

car1:accelerate(60)
car2:accelerate(75)
car1:brake(10)
```

**Output:**

```
Creating new vehicle: Lua Motors  Scriptster
Creating new vehicle: TableTech  Array GT
Lua Motors accelerating to: 60
TableTech accelerating to: 75
Lua Motors braking to: 50
```

The `Vehicle:new(...)` constructor provides a clean, consistent way to create properly initialized vehicle objects that automatically inherit methods from `Vehicle`. The `Vehicle.__index = Vehicle` line is a common idiom: it ensures that when `setmetatable(instance, self)` is called inside `Vehicle:new`, the metatable's `__index` field points back to the `Vehicle` table itself.

# Inheritance

OOP often involves creating specialized classes based on more general ones (e.g., a `Car` *is a* `Vehicle`, an `ElectricCar` *is a* `Car`). Lua's `__index` mechanism supports this kind of **inheritance** naturally.

To make `Car` inherit from `Vehicle`:

1. **Create the `Car` table:** This will hold methods specific to cars or override methods from `Vehicle`.
2. **Set `Car`'s metatable:** Make `Car` itself inherit from `Vehicle` so that if a method isn't found in `Car`, Lua looks in `Vehicle`. We do this using `setmetatable(Car, { __index = Vehicle })`.
3. **Define `Car`'s constructor (`Car:new`):** This usually needs to:
   - Create an instance table.
   - Set the instance's metatable to `{ __index = Car }` so it looks for methods in `Car` first.
   - Call the parent class's constructor (`Vehicle.new`) or initialization logic to set up the common vehicle properties.
   - Initialize car-specific properties.

164

4. **Add/Override Methods:** Define any new methods specific to Car or redefine methods inherited from Vehicle.

```lua
-- (Vehicle class definition from previous example)

-- 1. Create the Car subclass table
local Car = {}

-- 2. Set Car's metatable to inherit from Vehicle
setmetatable(Car, { __index = Vehicle })
-- This ensures Car itself behaves like a Vehicle, inheriting 'new', etc.
-- if needed, and allows method lookup chain: instance -> Car -> Vehicle.

-- 3. Define Car's constructor
function Car:new(make, model, color, numDoors)
  print("Creating new car:", make, model)
  -- Create instance table using Vehicle's constructor first
  -- Note: Calling the superclass method with '.' to pass 'self' (the Car table)
explicitly
  --       is one way, or just create the table and set metatable.
  --       Let's use a simpler approach here:
  local instance = Vehicle:new(make, model, color) -- Use Vehicle's initializer

  -- Set the instance's metatable to Car (overrides the one set by Vehicle:new)
  -- so method lookups start at Car.
  setmetatable(instance, { __index = Car })

  -- Initialize Car-specific properties
  instance.numDoors = numDoors or 4

  return instance
end

-- 4. Add/Override Methods
function Car:honk()
  print(self.make .. " says: Honk! Honk!")
end

-- Optional: Override accelerate if cars accelerate differently
-- function Car:accelerate(amount)
--    print(self.make .. " car accelerating...")
--    -- Call the parent's accelerate method explicitly if needed
--    Vehicle.accelerate(self, amount * 1.1) -- e.g., cars accelerate faster
--    -- Or rewrite acceleration logic entirely
-- end
```

```
-- --- Usage ---
local myLuxuryCar = Car:new("MetaMotors", "Sedan", "silver", 4)
local mySportsCar = Car:new("Lua Speedsters", "Racer", "yellow", 2)

myLuxuryCar:accelerate(70) -- Uses Vehicle:accelerate (as Car doesn't override
it)
mySportsCar:honk()         -- Uses Car:honk
myLuxuryCar:brake(30)      -- Uses Vehicle:brake

print(myLuxuryCar.make, "has", myLuxuryCar.numDoors, "doors.")
```

**Output:**

```
Creating new car: MetaMotors      Sedan
Creating new vehicle: MetaMotors  Sedan
Creating new car: Lua Speedsters Racer
Creating new vehicle: Lua Speedsters Racer
MetaMotors accelerating to: 70
Lua Speedsters says: Honk! Honk!
MetaMotors braking to: 40
MetaMotors has 4 doors.
```

Method lookup now follows the chain: myLuxuryCar -> Car -> Vehicle. The first
accelerate found is in Vehicle. The first honk found is in Car.

# Privacy and Encapsulation

**Encapsulation** is the bundling of data with the methods that operate on that data, and
restricting direct access to an object's internal state (often called information hiding or
privacy).

Lua has **no built-in mechanism** to enforce privacy like private or protected
keywords. All table fields are publicly accessible by default.

The widely accepted **convention** in the Lua community is to indicate "non-public"
members (those intended for internal use within the class or its subclasses) by prefix-
ing their names with a single underscore (_).

```
local Account = {}
Account.__index = Account

function Account:new(initialBalance)
  local instance = {}
```

```
  setmetatable(instance, self)
  instance._balance = initialBalance -- Convention: '_' indicates non-public
  return instance
end

function Account:deposit(amount)
  self._balance = self._balance + amount
end

function Account:withdraw(amount)
  if amount > self._balance then
    error("Insufficient funds")
  end
  self._balance = self._balance - amount
end

function Account:getBalance() -- Public accessor method
  return self._balance
end

-- Usage
local acc = Account:new(100)
acc:deposit(50)
-- print(acc._balance) -- POSSIBLE, but considered BAD PRACTICE to access
directly
print("Current balance:", acc:getBalance()) -- Preferred way
```

This underscore convention relies entirely on programmer discipline. It's a signal saying, "You probably shouldn't touch this directly from outside the object's own methods."

**Simulating True Privacy:** It *is* possible to achieve stronger encapsulation using closures (Chapter 5). You can define methods inside the constructor where they form closures over local variables holding the instance data. These local variables are then truly inaccessible from outside.

```
function createSecureAccount(initialBalance)
  local balance = initialBalance -- Truly local, inaccessible from outside

  local instance = {} -- The public interface table

  function instance:deposit(amount)
    balance = balance + amount
  end
```

```
  function instance:withdraw(amount)
    if amount > balance then error("Insufficient funds") end
    balance = balance - amount
  end

  function instance:getBalance()
    return balance
  end

  -- No metatable needed here for basic methods, but could be added
  -- for inheritance or operator overloading.
  return instance
end

local secureAcc = createSecureAccount(200)
secureAcc:deposit(25)
print(secureAcc:getBalance()) -- Output: 225
-- print(secureAcc.balance) -- Output: nil (The 'balance' variable is not in the
table)
```

This closure-based approach provides true privacy but can be more complex to set up, especially with inheritance, and might have slight performance implications compared to the standard metatable approach. For most typical OOP needs in Lua, the underscore convention combined with metatables is sufficient and more idiomatic.

# Multiple Inheritance (Briefly)

What if you want a class to inherit behavior from *more than one* parent class? Lua's basic __index = ParentTable only supports single inheritance directly.

Multiple inheritance can be achieved, but it introduces complexities (like the "diamond problem" – what happens if two parents provide methods with the same name?). A common Lua technique involves setting the __index metamethod to a **function**. This function receives the table and the missing key as arguments and can then implement a custom search strategy, looking through a list of parent tables in a defined order.

```
-- Simplified concept - NOT production code
local function searchParents(parents)
  return function(instance, key)
    for _, parent in ipairs(parents) do
      local value = parent[key]
      if value then return value end -- Found in a parent
```

```
    end
    return nil -- Not found in any parent
  end
end

local Flyer = { fly = function(self) print(self.name .. " is flying!") end }
local Swimmer = { swim = function(self) print(self.name .. " is swimming!")
end }

local Duck = { name = "Duck" }
-- Make Duck inherit from Flyer AND Swimmer
setmetatable(Duck, { __index = searchParents({ Flyer, Swimmer }) })

Duck:fly()  -- Output: Duck is flying!
Duck:swim() -- Output: Duck is swimming!
```

While possible, multiple inheritance can make class hierarchies confusing. Often, alternative design patterns like **composition** (where an object *has* instances of other objects and delegates tasks to them) or using **mixins** (tables of functions merged into a class) are considered cleaner solutions in Lua.

# Comparing Lua OOP to Other Languages

- **Flexibility vs. Rigidity:** Lua's table-based OOP is less rigid than compile-time class systems. You can add methods to individual objects, change an object's "class" (by changing its metatable) at runtime, and easily implement prototype-based inheritance.
- **Simplicity (Core Language):** The core language remains simple; OOP is built *on top* of existing features (tables, functions, metatables), not added as separate complex syntax.
- **Explicit Mechanisms:** Understanding __index and metatables is essential. The magic is less hidden than in some languages with dedicated class syntax.
- **Convention over Enforcement:** Concepts like privacy rely heavily on programmer convention rather than language enforcement.

# Chapter Summary

This chapter demonstrated that while Lua lacks built-in class syntax, it provides all the necessary tools to implement object-oriented programming paradigms effectively. You learned how to represent objects and classes using tables, how the colon operator (:) simplifies method definition and calls by handling the self parameter implicitly, and how the `__index` metamethod is the key to linking instances to proto-type/class tables for method lookup and single inheritance. We explored the common constructor pattern (`Class:new`) for creating instances and saw how inheritance hier-archies can be built by chaining `__index` lookups through metatables. We also dis-cussed privacy conventions (_) versus true encapsulation with closures and briefly touched upon the complexities and alternatives to multiple inheritance. Lua's approach to OOP is flexible, powerful, and relies fundamentally on the core concepts of tables and metatables you've learned previously.

Now that you've seen how Lua handles common programming structures and paradigms, let's look at where Lua is commonly put to use in real-world scenarios in the next chapter.

# 16

# Lua in the Real World

Having explored Lua's data structures, control flow, functions, object-oriented patterns (Chapter 15), and standard libraries (Chapter 12), you might be wondering: where does all this theory meet practice? Where is Lua actually making a difference out in the world? While some languages dominate specific niches, Lua's strength lies in its remarkable versatility. Its combination of simplicity, speed, small size, and unparalleled ease of integration makes it a valuable tool across a surprisingly diverse range of applications. This chapter shines a spotlight on some of the key domains where Lua has found significant success, demonstrating its practical value beyond the fundamentals.

## Lua as an Extension Language

Perhaps the most common and defining role for Lua is as an **extension** or **scripting** language embedded within larger applications written in compiled languages like C or C++. This was, after all, one of its primary design goals, as discussed in Chapter 1.

### Why Embed Lua?

Imagine you've built a complex scientific simulation, a graphic design tool, or a server application in C++. You want to allow users (or other developers on your team) to customize its behavior, automate repetitive tasks, or add new features without needing to recompile the entire core application. Embedding Lua provides a perfect solution:

- **Flexibility:** Users can write simple Lua scripts to control aspects of the main application.
- **Safety:** The Lua environment runs within a sandbox. Scripts typically cannot crash the entire host application unless explicitly allowed dangerous operations.
- **Rapid Prototyping:** New features or logic can often be developed much faster in Lua than in C++.
- **Accessibility:** Users don't need complex C++ build environments; they can often just edit text-based Lua scripts.

The C application uses the Lua C API (Chapter 14) to create a Lua state, expose specific C functions or data structures to the Lua environment (e.g., `hostApp.setColor("red")`), and then load and run Lua scripts.

## Use Cases for Embedded Lua

- **Configuration Files:** Instead of plain text files or complex formats like XML/ YAML, some applications use Lua scripts for configuration. This allows for dynamic settings, conditional logic, and computation directly within the configuration itself.

```lua
-- config.lua (Example Configuration)
local is_production = os.getenv("APP_ENV") == "production"

settings = {
  window_title = "My Application v1.2",
  graphics = {
    resolution_x = 1920,
    resolution_y = 1080,
    fullscreen = is_production, -- Use logic in config!
    vsync = true
  },
  network = {
    server_ip = is_production and "10.0.1.5" or "127.0.0.1",
    port = 8080
  },
  -- Define a function the host app can call
  on_startup = function()
    print("Configuration loaded! Production mode:", is_production)
  end
}
-- The C++ application would load this file, execute it,
-- and then read values from the global 'settings' table.
```

- **Plugin Systems:** Many applications allow third-party developers to extend their functionality through plugins. Lua is a popular choice for plugin scripting because it's relatively easy to learn and secure to run. The host application defines an API that Lua plugins can call to interact with the application's core features.

- **Specific Examples:**
  - **Adobe Lightroom:** Uses Lua for developing plugins to automate photo processing tasks, add UI elements, and integrate with web services.
  - **Redis:** Allows complex atomic operations and server-side scripting using Lua procedures.
  - **Neovim / Vim:** Modern text editors that leverage Lua extensively for configuration and plugin development, offering significant performance benefits over older scripting methods.
  - **Wireshark:** The network protocol analyzer uses Lua for writing custom protocol "dissectors" and post-processing scripts.
  - **Nginx (via OpenResty):** While also a web server use case, OpenResty fundamentally embeds Lua deeply into the Nginx request processing cycle.

# Powering Game Development

Game development is arguably Lua's most visible and successful domain. Its characteristics make it an almost perfect fit for many aspects of game creation.

## Why Lua in Games?

- **Rapid Iteration:** Game logic (like AI behavior, quest progression, weapon stats, UI flow) often requires frequent tweaking during development. Modifying Lua scripts is much faster than recompiling large C++ codebases, allowing designers and scripters to experiment and iterate quickly.
- **Ease of Use:** Lua's simple syntax makes it accessible to team members who aren't hardcore C++ programmers, like game designers or level scripters.
- **Performance:** While C++ handles the heavy lifting of the graphics engine and physics, Lua is generally fast enough for the scripting layer that controls *what* the engine does. LuaJIT (a high-performance implementation of Lua 5.1) is often used for even greater speed.

- **Embeddability & Small Footprint:** Game engines (often written in C++) can easily embed Lua, and its small size is advantageous, especially on resource-constrained platforms like mobile devices or consoles.
- **Modding:** Exposing a Lua API allows players to create modifications ("mods") for games, extending their lifespan and building vibrant communities (e.g., World of Warcraft UI addons).

## Scripting Game Logic

Lua is commonly used to script:

- **Artificial Intelligence (AI):** Defining how non-player characters (NPCs) react to the player, make decisions, and navigate the world.
- **User Interface (UI):** Handling button clicks, displaying information, managing menus, and animating UI elements.
- **Gameplay Events:** Defining what happens when specific events occur (e.g., player enters a region, completes an objective, picks up an item).
- **Quests and Dialogue:** Scripting the flow of quests, conditions for advancement, and character conversations.
- **Weapon/Item Behavior:** Defining damage, effects, cooldowns, and special abilities.

## Popular Engines and Games

- **Roblox:** Uses its own optimized dialect, Luau, enabling millions of users to create and share interactive experiences. This is one of the largest deployments of Lua-like technology in the world.
- **Defold Engine:** A free, lightweight engine developed by King (and later the Defold Foundation) that uses Lua as its primary scripting language.
- **LÖVE (or Love2D):** A popular open-source framework for making 2D games in Lua, known for its simplicity and supportive community.
- **Solar2D (formerly Corona SDK):** Another mature framework using Lua, often favoured for mobile game and app development.
- **World of Warcraft:** Famous for its extensive UI modification capabilities powered by Lua. Players write addons to customize almost every aspect of the game's interface.
- **Civilization Series:** Uses Lua for various scripting tasks, including AI and UI elements.
- ...and countless others, ranging from small indie titles to large AAA productions, often using Lua internally even if it's not publicly advertised.

# Lua on the Web

While languages like JavaScript (Node.js), Python (Django/Flask), Ruby (Rails), or PHP dominate general web development, Lua has carved out a significant niche in **high-performance web infrastructure**.

## Server-Side Scripting with OpenResty

The most prominent player here is **OpenResty**. It's not technically a Lua web server itself, but rather a highly enhanced web platform built by bundling the standard Nginx web server with a powerful LuaJIT integration.

- **Nginx + LuaJIT:** OpenResty allows developers to write Lua scripts that run directly within Nginx's efficient, event-driven architecture. These scripts can intercept different phases of the HTTP request/response lifecycle.
- **Use Cases:** Developers use OpenResty/Lua for:
    - Building high-performance dynamic web applications and APIs.
    - Creating sophisticated API gateways (like Kong, which is built on OpenResty).
    - Implementing dynamic routing, authentication, and request/response transformation logic.
    - Developing Web Application Firewalls (WAFs).
    - Real-time analytics and request logging.
- **Advantages:**
    - **Performance:** Leverages Nginx's speed and LuaJIT's near-C performance for scripted logic.
    - **Concurrency:** Makes excellent use of Nginx's non-blocking I/O model, often combined with Lua coroutines (managed by libraries within OpenResty) to handle tens of thousands of concurrent connections efficiently without the heavy resource usage of traditional threaded servers.

## Lua Web Frameworks

While OpenResty provides the foundation, several web frameworks have been built on top of it (or run independently) to offer higher-level structures (like Model-View-Controller patterns) for building web applications in Lua:

- **Lapis:** A popular framework for Lua/OpenResty, emphasizing speed and providing tools for routing, HTML templating, database access, etc. (http://leafo.net/lapis/)
- **Sailor:** Another MVC framework for Lua. (https://sailorproject.org/)

Lua on the web shines particularly where performance and high concurrency under heavy load are critical requirements.

# Other Interesting Use Cases

Lua's flexibility leads to its adoption in various other areas:

- **Text Processing:** Lua's powerful `string` library, especially its pattern matching (Chapter 8), makes it quite capable for tasks involving text manipulation, data extraction from logs, simple parsing, and format conversion.
- **System Administration:** For writing small, fast automation scripts, Lua can be an alternative to shell scripts, Perl, or Python, especially when dependencies need to be minimal or integration with a C application is required.
- **Embedded Systems:** Although C remains dominant due to its direct hardware control, Lua's extremely small footprint (the core interpreter can be under 200KB) and portability make it a viable option for scripting on some resource-constrained microcontrollers or embedded Linux systems where a scripting layer is beneficial. Projects like eLua specifically target these platforms.
- **Scientific Computing:** While languages like Python (with NumPy/SciPy) or specialized languages like R or Julia are more common, Lua is sometimes used as a "glue" language in scientific computing environments, orchestrating workflows or providing scripting interfaces for large simulation codes often written in Fortran or C/C++.

# Brief Case Studies (Scenarios)

Let's revisit some earlier concepts with these applications in mind:

1. **Game Mod Configuration:** A game exposes a Lua API. A player wants to change the color of a specific UI element. They might write a simple config.lua script loaded by the game's addon system:

```
-- Mod config.lua
```

```lua
local ui_elements = HostGame.GetUIElements() -- Call C++ function
exposed to Lua
local health_bar = ui_elements.HealthBar

if health_bar then
  health_bar:SetColor(0.8, 0.1, 0.1, 0.9) -- Call method on object
exposed from C++
  health_bar:SetTextFormat("{value} / {max_value}")
end
```

*Uses tables, potentially userdata/metatables from C++, function calls.*

2. **Dynamic Web Server Routing (OpenResty):** A web server needs to route requests based on a user's region, determined by their IP address. An Open-Resty Lua script could handle this:

```lua
-- access_phase.lua (Runs early in Nginx request processing)
local geo_lookup = require("geoip_lib") -- Hypothetical geoip module
local request_ip = ngx.var.remote_addr    -- Get request IP from Nginx
variable

local region = geo_lookup.get_region(request_ip)

if region == "EU" then
  ngx.var.backend_server = "eu_server_pool" -- Set Nginx variable for
upstream
elseif region == "US" then
  ngx.var.backend_server = "us_server_pool"
else
  ngx.var.backend_server = "default_server_pool"
end
-- Nginx continues processing, using the 'backend_server' variable
```

*Uses modules,* ngx *API (specific to OpenResty), conditional logic.*

3. **Custom Data Validation (Embedded):** An application allows users to define validation rules for data entry using Lua.

```lua
-- validation_rule.lua
function validate_product_code(code)
  -- Rule: Must be 8 chars, start with 'P', end with a digit
  if type(code) ~= "string" then return false, "Code must be a string"
end
  if #code ~= 8 then return false, "Code must be 8 characters long" end
```

```
  -- Use string patterns (Chapter 8)
  local pattern = "^P%w+%d$" -- Starts with P, any alphanumeric, ends
with digit
  if string.match(code, pattern) then
    return true -- Valid
  else
    return false, "Invalid format (must be PxxxxxxD)"
  end
end
-- Host application calls validate_product_code(userInput) using C API
```

*Uses functions, type checking, string library, patterns.*

# Chapter Summary

Lua is far more than just an academic exercise; it's a pragmatic language solving real-world problems across diverse industries. We've seen its crucial role as an **extension language**, allowing customization and scripting in applications ranging from graphic design software to databases and text editors. Its dominance in **game development** for scripting logic, AI, and UI is undeniable, driven by its speed, simplicity, and ease of embedding. In the **web world**, Lua shines in high-performance scenarios, particularly through platforms like OpenResty. We also touched upon its utility in text processing, system administration, and even specialized embedded systems. These practical applications demonstrate Lua's value proposition: a small, fast, portable, and easily integrated language ideal for extending larger systems or building specialized, efficient applications.

Successfully implementing Lua in these real-world projects requires more than just knowing the syntax; it demands writing code that is clean, readable, maintainable, testable, and efficient. In the next chapter, we'll focus on exactly these aspects, covering coding style, debugging techniques, testing strategies, and performance considerations to help you write high-quality Lua code.

# 17

# Writing Quality Code

You've journeyed through Lua's core features, explored its powerful tables and metatables, learned how to organize code with modules (Chapter 10), handle errors (Chapter 9), and even peeked at interacting with C (Chapter 14) and its real-world applications (Chapter 16). Knowing the language features is essential, but writing code that *works* is only the first hurdle. To build robust, scalable, and collaborative projects, you need to write *quality* code – code that is not just functional but also clear, easy to understand, simple to modify, and demonstrably correct. This chapter focuses on the craft of Lua programming: adopting good coding style, effectively finding and fixing bugs (debugging), verifying correctness through testing, and considering performance when it truly matters. These practices elevate your code from a simple script to professional-quality software.

## The Importance of Good Code

Why should you care about code quality beyond just making it run?

- **Readability:** Code is read far more often than it is written, both by others and by your future self. Clear, well-structured code is easier to understand, reducing the mental effort required to figure out what it does. Think of it like reading a well-formatted book versus deciphering hastily scribbled notes.
- **Maintainability:** Software evolves. Requirements change, bugs are found, features are added. Code that is easy to understand is also easier and safer to

modify. Poorly written code can turn simple changes into complex, risky operations.
- **Collaboration:** If you're working on a team (or even sharing code with others), a consistent and readable style is paramount. It allows everyone to understand and contribute to the codebase more effectively.
- **Debugging:** Clean code is often easier to debug. When logic is straightforward and well-organized, pinpointing the source of an error becomes much simpler.

Investing time in writing quality code pays off significantly in the long run, saving time, effort, and frustration.

# Lua Coding Style and Conventions

While Lua's syntax is flexible, following established conventions makes code more readable and predictable for everyone familiar with Lua. **Consistency** is the most important principle – pick a style and stick to it throughout your project.

## Naming Conventions

- **Variables and Functions:** Choose descriptive names that clearly indicate the purpose. `player_score` or `calculateTotal` is much better than `ps` or `calc`. Common casing styles include:
  - `camelCase`: `playerName`, `maxHealth`, `getUserInput` (often seen in application code).
  - `snake_case`: `player_name`, `max_health`, `get_user_input` (often seen in libraries, especially those interfacing with C).
  - Neither is officially "better"; choose one style for your project and apply it consistently.
- **Constants:** For values that are intended to remain constant, the convention is to use all uppercase letters with underscores as separators: `MAX_PLAYERS`, `DEFAULT_TIMEOUT`. (Lua doesn't enforce constants, this is purely a convention for readability).
- **Boolean Variables:** Often benefit from names starting with `is`, `has`, or `should` (e.g., `isActive`, `hasCollided`).
- **Module Tables:** Often named `M` or a short, descriptive name within the module file (as seen in Chapter 10).

# Indentation and Spacing

- **Indentation:** Use spaces (typically 2 or 4 per indentation level) or tabs consistently to show code structure within blocks (`if, for, while, function,` etc.). Mixing spaces and tabs is generally discouraged as it leads to inconsistent appearance in different editors.
- **Spaces:** Use spaces around operators (`a + b` not `a+b`) and after commas (`func(a, b)` not `func(a,b)`) to improve readability.
- **Blank Lines:** Use blank lines sparingly to separate logical chunks of code within a function or file, improving visual organization.

```
-- Good indentation and spacing
local function calculateDamage(baseDamage, defense, criticalHit)
  local effectiveDamage = baseDamage - defense
  if effectiveDamage < 0 then
    effectiveDamage = 0 -- Can't deal negative damage
  end

  if criticalHit then
    effectiveDamage = effectiveDamage * 2
  end

  return effectiveDamage
end


-- Less readable version
function calculateDamage(baseDamage,defense,criticalHit)
local effectiveDamage=baseDamage-defense
if effectiveDamage<0 then
effectiveDamage=0
end
if criticalHit then
effectiveDamage=effectiveDamage*2
end
return effectiveDamage
end
```

# Line Length

Aim to keep lines of code relatively short, often around **80 characters**. This standard stems from historical terminal widths but remains practical because:

- It avoids horizontal scrolling in most editors and code review tools.
- It encourages breaking down complex statements into simpler ones.

- It generally improves readability.

If a statement becomes too long, break it down or wrap it logically:

```
-- Long line
local average = (score1 + score2 + score3 + score4 + score5 + score6) / 6

-- Better: Break it down or wrap
local totalScore = score1 + score2 + score3 + score4 + score5 + score6
local average = totalScore / 6

-- Or wrap logically (alignment helps)
local message = "Player " .. player.name ..
                " achieved level " .. player.level ..
                " with score " .. player.score .. "."
```

## Use `local` Variables Generously

As stressed multiple times (Chapters 2, 5, 10), **always declare variables with** `local` unless you specifically need a global variable (which should be rare). This:

- Prevents accidental modification of variables from other parts of the code.
- Improves performance slightly, as Lua can access locals faster than globals.
- Makes code easier to understand by limiting the scope where a variable is active.
- Helps the garbage collector (Chapter 13) by allowing variables to go out of scope and become unreachable more readily.

## Commenting Wisely

Comments explain the code to human readers. Write comments to clarify the *why*, not just the *what* (if the code itself is clear).

- **Explain Complex Logic:** If an algorithm or calculation is non-obvious, explain the reasoning behind it.
- **Clarify Intent:** Explain the purpose of a tricky piece of code or why a particular approach was chosen over another.
- **Document Assumptions:** If your code relies on specific preconditions or external states, document them.
- **Module/Function Headers:** Use comments at the top of files or before functions to explain their overall purpose, parameters, and return values (tools like LDoc use specific comment formats for this).

- **Avoid Obvious Comments:** Don't comment on things the code already says clearly.

  ```
  -- Bad comment:
  local i = i + 1 -- Increment i

  -- Good comment:
  -- Apply gravity adjustment based on planetary mass (Newton's Law)
  local force = G * mass1 * mass2 / (distance ^ 2)
  ```

- **Keep Comments Updated:** If you change the code, make sure you update the comments accordingly! Outdated comments are worse than no comments.

# Finding and Fixing Bugs

Even with careful coding, bugs happen. **Debugging** is the process of finding and fixing errors in your code.

## Beyond `print`

The humble `print()` statement is often the first debugging tool programmers reach for, and it can be surprisingly effective for simple cases. You can insert `print(variable)` or `print(type(variable))` calls to trace the state of your program.

- **Tip:** Use `io.stderr:write(...)` for debug messages. This often writes to a separate stream from your program's normal output (`print` usually writes to `io.stdout`), making it easier to distinguish debug information, especially if your program produces a lot of standard output or if standard output is being redirected. `io.stderr:write` also doesn't add tabs or newlines automatically, giving you more control.

  ```
  local function process(data)
    io.stderr:write(string.format("DEBUG: Processing data: %q\n", data))
    -- ... processing logic ...
    local result = data * 2 -- Potential error if data is not a number!
    io.stderr:write(string.format("DEBUG: Result: %s\n",
  tostring(result)))
    return result
  end
  ```

- Combine `print` with `tostring` or `string.format("%q", ...)` to handle different data types gracefully and see distinctions between `nil`, `"nil"`, numbers, etc.

## Leveraging Error Messages and Stack Traces

As mentioned in Chapter 9, pay close attention to Lua's error messages and stack traces. They pinpoint the location (file and line) and the type of runtime error, and the trace shows the function call sequence leading up to it. This is often enough to identify the source of the problem. Use `debug.traceback()` within `pcall` or `xpcall` error handlers to capture this information programmatically for logging.

## Using the `debug` Library Intelligently

While generally avoided in production code, the `debug` library (Chapter 12) offers powerful tools during development:

- `debug.getinfo(level or func, "Sl")`: Get source and line number information for a specific stack level or function.
- `debug.getlocal(level, index)` / `debug.getupvalue(func, index)`: Inspect the names and values of local variables or upvalues at specific points in the call stack. This can be invaluable when an error occurs deep within nested calls.
- Remember `debug.traceback()` for generating stack traces on demand.

## External Debuggers

For more complex scenarios, `print` debugging can become tedious. Visual debuggers provide a much more powerful experience:

- **Breakpoints:** Set points in your code where execution should pause.
- **Stepping:** Execute code line-by-line (`step over`, `step into`, `step out`).
- **Variable Inspection:** Examine the values of local and global variables (and often upvalues) while the program is paused.
- **Call Stack Inspection:** View the current function call stack.

Popular Lua debuggers include:

- **ZeroBrane Studio:** A lightweight Lua IDE with a built-in debugger.
- **VS Code Extensions:** Several extensions provide debugging support for Lua within Visual Studio Code (often using protocols like Debug Adapter Protocol).

- Debugging embedded Lua often requires integration with the host application's debugger (e.g., using C API calls to trigger breakpoints or inspect the Lua state from GDB/Visual Studio).

Using a proper debugger can drastically reduce the time it takes to find and fix complex bugs.

# Ensuring Correctness

Debugging fixes errors *after* they occur. **Testing** is the proactive process of verifying that your code behaves correctly under various conditions, aiming to catch bugs *before* they reach users.

## Why Test?

- **Confidence:** Tests provide confidence that your code works as intended.
- **Regression Prevention:** When you fix a bug or add a feature, tests ensure you haven't accidentally broken existing functionality elsewhere (these are called **regression tests**).
- **Design Improvement:** Thinking about how to test code often forces you to write it in a more modular and testable way (e.g., breaking large functions into smaller, testable units).
- **Documentation:** Tests serve as executable documentation, demonstrating how your code is supposed to be used and what results are expected.

## Unit Testing Concepts

The most common form of testing is **unit testing**. A unit test focuses on verifying a small, isolated piece of code (a "unit"), typically a single function or method, in isolation from the rest of the system.

- **Arrange:** Set up any necessary preconditions or input data for the unit being tested.
- **Act:** Execute the unit of code (e.g., call the function).
- **Assert:** Check if the result (return values, side effects, state changes) matches the expected outcome. Use `assert` (Chapter 9) or assertion functions provided by testing frameworks.

# Lua Testing Frameworks

While you can write simple tests using just `assert`, dedicated testing frameworks provide structure, test discovery, reporting, and helpful assertion functions. Popular choices in the Lua ecosystem include:

- **Busted:** ([http://olivinelabs.com/busted/](http://olivinelabs.com/busted/)) A widely used, feature-rich framework inspired by RSpec (Ruby). It supports Behavior-Driven Development (BDD) style (`describe`/`it` blocks) and provides many built-in assertions.
- **Telescope:** Another testing framework option.
- Others exist, often tailored to specific environments (like game engines).

Example using Busted syntax (conceptual):

```lua
-- Assuming strutils.lua from Chapter 10 exists
describe("String Utilities Module (strutils)", function()
  local strutils = require("strutils") -- Arrange: Load the module

  describe("isEmpty()", function()
    it("should return true for nil", function()
      assert.is_true(strutils.isEmpty(nil)) -- Assert
    end)

    it("should return true for empty string", function()
      assert.is_true(strutils.isEmpty("")) -- Assert
    end)

    it("should return false for non-empty string", function()
      assert.is_false(strutils.isEmpty("hello")) -- Assert
    end)

    it("should return false for numbers", function()
      assert.is_false(strutils.isEmpty(123)) -- Assert
    end)
  end)

  describe("repeatString()", function()
    it("should repeat the string correctly", function()
      assert.are.equal("ababab", strutils.repeatString("ab", 3)) -- Assert
    end)

    it("should return empty string for 0 repetitions", function()
      assert.are.equal("", strutils.repeatString("abc", 0)) -- Assert
    end)

    -- Busted also provides ways to assert that an error occurs
```

```
    it("should error on invalid input", function()
      assert.error(function() strutils.repeatString("a", -1) end)
    end)
  end)
end)
```

Running busted in the terminal would discover and run these tests, reporting successes and failures.

## Writing Testable Code

- **Pure Functions:** Functions that always return the same output for the same input and have no side effects are easiest to test.
- **Dependency Injection:** Instead of having a function directly depend on global state or hard-coded external services (like network requests or file I/O), pass those dependencies in as arguments (often as tables or functions). In tests, you can then pass in "mock" or "stub" versions of these dependencies that provide controlled behavior without needing real network or file access.
- **Small Units:** Break down large, complex functions into smaller, focused functions, each performing a testable sub-task.

# Performance Tuning

Lua is generally fast, but sometimes performance becomes critical.

## Don't Optimize Prematurely

> "Premature optimization is the root of all evil." - Donald Knuth (attributed)

**Write clear, correct, and readable code first.** Only optimize if:

1. You **know** you have a performance problem.
2. You have **measured** (profiled) your code and identified the actual **bottlenecks**.

Optimizing code that isn't a bottleneck wastes time and often makes the code harder to read and maintain for little or no real gain.

## Measure!

Use tools to find out where your code is spending most of its time:

- `os.clock()`: For basic timing of specific code blocks.
- **Profiling Tools:** Lua has built-in profiling capabilities (`debug.sethook` with the `"l"` hook can count line executions) and external profilers exist (e.g., built into ZeroBrane Studio, standalone profilers). These tools give a detailed breakdown of time spent in each function.

# Common Areas for Optimization (After Profiling)

- **Table Creation:** Creating many tables inside tight loops can pressure the GC. Reuse tables where possible if profiling shows table creation is a bottleneck.
- **String Concatenation:** Concatenating many strings in a loop using `..` can be inefficient because each `..` creates a new intermediate string. For many concatenations, it's often faster to insert the strings into a table and use `table.concat` at the end.

```
-- Slower in a loop with many iterations:
-- local result = ""
-- for i = 1, 10000 do result = result .. some_string end

-- Often faster:
local parts = {}
for i = 1, 10000 do parts[i] = some_string end
local result = table.concat(parts)
```

- **Localize Globals:** Accessing local variables is faster than accessing global variables. If you use a global function (like `math.sin`) or module table repeatedly inside a performance-critical loop, localize it outside the loop:

```
-- Slower:
-- for i = 1, 100000 do local y = math.sin(i * 0.01) end

-- Faster:
local sin = math.sin -- Localize the function lookup
for i = 1, 100000 do local y = sin(i * 0.01) end
```

- **Algorithms and Data Structures:** Often, the biggest gains come from choosing a more efficient algorithm or a data structure better suited to the task, rather than micro-optimizing Lua code.
- **LuaJIT:** For computationally intensive Lua code, consider using LuaJIT (http://luajit.org/). It's a separate, highly optimizing Just-In-Time compiler for

Lua 5.1 (with some features backported) that can provide dramatic speedups, often approaching C-level performance for numerical code.
- **Move to C:** For the absolute most demanding parts of your application, implement them as C functions callable from Lua using the C API (Chapter 14).

# Writing Defensively

Write code that anticipates potential problems:

- **Validate Function Arguments:** Use `assert` or `if` checks at the beginning of functions (especially public API functions) to ensure arguments are of the expected type and within valid ranges. Fail fast if inputs are invalid.
- **Handle** `nil`: Be aware of operations that can return `nil` (table lookups, potentially failing functions) and check for it before trying to use the result, especially before indexing (`if value then print(value.field) end`).
- **Graceful Error Handling:** Use `pcall` where appropriate (Chapter 9) to handle potential runtime errors from external sources or operations that might fail under specific conditions.

# Documentation Matters

Good code includes good documentation.

- **Public APIs:** Document the functions and variables exposed by your modules. Explain what they do, what parameters they expect (types, purpose), and what they return.
- **Internal Comments:** Use comments to explain complex or non-obvious parts of the implementation (as discussed under Style).
- **Documentation Generators:** Tools like **LDoc** (https://github.com/lunarmodules/LDoc) can automatically generate HTML documentation from specially formatted comments in your Lua code, similar to Javadoc or Doxygen. Adopting a documentation generator encourages consistent documentation practices.

# Chapter Summary

This chapter transitioned from simply knowing Lua to crafting quality Lua code. We emphasized the importance of readability, maintainability, and collaboration, driven by consistent **coding style** (naming, spacing, locality, comments). You learned practical **debugging** strategies beyond basic `print` statements, including leveraging error messages, stack traces, and the potential of dedicated debuggers. We introduced the crucial practice of **testing**, focusing on unit tests, the Arrange-Act-Assert pattern, and the role of testing frameworks like Busted. We discussed **performance tuning**, stressing the importance of measuring before optimizing and covering common areas like table/string handling and localization, also mentioning LuaJIT and C integration as advanced options. Finally, we touched upon defensive programming and the value of clear documentation. Applying these principles consistently will significantly improve the quality, robustness, and longevity of your Lua projects.

You've now covered the breadth of the Lua language and the practices for using it effectively. Our final chapter will briefly recap the journey and point you towards resources for continuing your exploration of the vibrant Lua ecosystem.

# 18

# Your Lua Journey Continues

And just like that, you've navigated the landscape of Lua programming, from the first `print` statement to the intricacies of metatables, coroutines, and even the C API! Take a moment to appreciate how far you've come. You started with the basic building blocks and progressively assembled them into a comprehensive understanding of how Lua works and how to wield its elegant power. This final chapter isn't about learning new features, but about consolidating what you've learned, celebrating your progress, and charting a course for your continued exploration of the Lua universe. Think of it as reaching a scenic overlook – a chance to look back at the path traveled and gaze forward at the exciting possibilities ahead.

## You've Learned a Lot!

Let's briefly retrace the key landmarks on your Lua journey through this book:

- You started with the fundamentals: Lua's philosophy, setting up your environment, basic syntax, variables, and the core data types like `nil`, `boolean`, `number`, and `string` (Chapters 1-2).

- You learned to control the flow of your programs using operators, expressions, conditional logic with `if`, `elseif`, `else`, and repetition with `while`, `repeat`, and `for` loops (Chapters 3-4).
- You mastered functions – defining them, passing arguments, getting multiple return values, understanding scope (`local`!), and exploring the power of first-class functions, closures, and recursion (Chapter 5).
- You dove deep into Lua's cornerstone: the versatile `table`, learning how to use it as arrays, dictionaries, and how to iterate over it with `pairs` and `ipairs` (Chapter 6).
- You unlocked table superpowers with metatables and metamethods like `__index`, `__newindex`, `__add`, and `__tostring`, enabling operator overloading and custom behaviors (Chapter 7).
- You tackled text manipulation using the `string` library, including powerful pattern matching (Chapter 8).
- You learned to write more robust programs by anticipating and handling errors using `pcall`, `xpcall`, `assert`, and `error` (Chapter 9).
- You discovered how to structure larger projects using modules and packages with `require` (Chapter 10).
- You explored Lua's unique approach to cooperative multitasking with coroutines (`yield`, `resume`, `wrap`) (Chapter 11).
- You toured the essential tools provided by Lua's standard libraries: `math`, `os`, `io`, `table`, `debug`, and `utf8` (Chapter 12).
- You understood the principles of automatic memory management via Garbage Collection, including weak tables and finalizers (Chapter 13).
- You opened the door to extending Lua's capabilities and embedding it in other applications by learning the basics of the Lua C API and the virtual stack (Chapter 14).
- You saw how Lua's flexible features allow you to implement object-oriented programming patterns (Chapter 15).
- You discovered where Lua makes its mark in the real world, from game development and web servers to application scripting (Chapter 16).
- Finally, you learned about the craft of writing quality code through consistent style, effective debugging, essential testing, and mindful performance considerations (Chapter 17).

That's a significant amount of knowledge! You now possess a solid foundation in Lua programming.

# The Vibrant Lua Community

Programming languages are more than just syntax and semantics; they are living ecosystems supported by communities of developers. Engaging with the Lua community is one of the best ways to continue learning, get help when you're stuck, and discover new libraries and techniques.

Here are some key places to connect:

- **The Official Lua Website ([lua.org](lua.org))**: The source of truth. Here you'll find the official documentation (including the Reference Manual), source code downloads, history, and links to other resources.
- **Lua Mailing List ([lua.org/lua-l.html](lua.org/lua-l.html))**: This is the primary, long-standing forum for discussion among Lua developers, including the language creators. It's a great place to ask technical questions (after searching the archives!), discuss language design, and see announcements.
- **Lua Workshop ([www.lua.org/wshop/](www.lua.org/wshop/))**: An annual event where Lua developers from around the world gather to present talks and discuss their work with Lua. Presentations from past workshops are often available online.
- **Online Forums and Communities:**
  - **Stack Overflow:** Has a large number of Lua-related questions and answers. Remember to search before asking!
  - **Reddit:** The `r/lua` subreddit is an active community for news, questions, and showing off projects.
  - **Discord Servers:** Various servers dedicated to Lua or specific frameworks (like LÖVE, Defold) exist, offering real-time chat and help.

Don't hesitate to participate. Asking well-formulated questions, sharing your solutions, and helping others are great ways to deepen your own understanding.

# Essential Resources

Beyond community interaction, certain resources are indispensable for any serious Lua developer:

- **Programming in Lua (PiL):** Written by Roberto Ierusalimschy, Lua's chief architect, this is the definitive book on Lua. It provides deep insights into the language design and practical usage. While you may need to purchase the latest edition covering recent versions, earlier editions (often covering Lua 5.0 or 5.1) are available freely online ([www.lua.org/pil/](www.lua.org/pil/)) and still cover the core concepts extremely well. This book you've just read aims to complement PiL, offering a different path through the material. Reading PiL is highly recommended for a deeper dive.

- **Lua Reference Manual** (www.lua.org/manual/): This is the official, precise specification of the Lua language and its standard libraries for a specific version. It's less of a tutorial and more of a technical reference – invaluable when you need the exact definition of how a function behaves or the precise syntax rules. Keep the manual for your Lua version handy!
- **LuaRocks** (luarocks.org): Just as Python has Pip and Node.js has npm, Lua has LuaRocks – the primary package manager for Lua modules. LuaRocks allows you to easily discover, install, and manage thousands of third-party libraries ("rocks") created by the community, covering everything from web frameworks and database drivers to data structures and game development tools. Learning to use LuaRocks is essential for leveraging the broader Lua ecosystem.

# The Evolution of Lua

Lua is not static; it continues to evolve, guided by its core principles of simplicity, efficiency, and portability. You'll encounter different versions of Lua (e.g., 5.1, 5.2, 5.3, 5.4, and future versions). While the core language remains remarkably stable, later versions introduce subtle but useful changes and additions:

- **Lua 5.1:** A long-lived and influential version, forming the basis for LuaJIT.
- **Lua 5.2:** Introduced _ENV for managing environments (affecting global variable access), yieldable pcall/metamethods, and bitwise operations.
- **Lua 5.3:** Introduced an official integer subtype for numbers, the utf8 library, bitwise operators, and changes to float/integer division.
- **Lua 5.4:** Introduced a new generational garbage collector mode, new toclose semantics for resource management, and const/close variable attributes.

You don't need to memorize every difference, but be aware that code written for one version might require minor adjustments for another, especially concerning features introduced later.

Also critically important is **LuaJIT** (luajit.org). While based on the Lua 5.1 language specification (with some backported features), LuaJIT uses a sophisticated Just-In-Time compiler to achieve significantly higher performance, often approaching C speeds, especially for numerical and repetitive code. It's widely used in game development (like Defold) and web infrastructure (like OpenResty) where performance is paramount. If you need maximum speed from Lua, LuaJIT is the tool to investigate.

# Contributing Back

As you become more proficient, consider contributing back to the Lua community:

- Help others on mailing lists or forums.
- Report bugs clearly to the Lua team or library authors.
- Write your own useful modules and publish them on LuaRocks.
- Contribute documentation or examples for existing projects.
- Participate in discussions about the language's future.

# Keep Coding! Project Ideas

The best way to solidify your knowledge and continue learning is to **build things**! Here are a few ideas for small projects to practice your Lua skills:

1. **Simple Text Adventure Game:** Use tables to represent rooms and items, functions for player actions (`go north`, `take item`), `io.read` for input, and `print` for descriptions.
2. **Configuration File Loader:** Write a module that can load a `.lua` configuration file (like the one shown in Chapter 16), validate its contents, and provide access to the settings.
3. **Command-Line Utility:** Create a script that performs a useful task from the terminal, like renaming files in a directory based on a pattern (`os`, `string` libraries), calculating word counts in text files (`io`, `string`), or fetching simple data from a web API (requires an external HTTP library via LuaRocks, like `lua-requests` or `lua-cURL`).
4. **Experiment with a Game Framework:** Download LÖVE ([love2d.org](love2d.org)) or Defold ([defold.com](defold.com)) and try making a simple 2D game (like Pong, Snake, or Asteroids). This is a great way to apply Lua in a fun, visual context.
5. **Basic C Integration:** Try writing a very simple C function (like one that adds two numbers) and make it callable from Lua using the C API techniques from Chapter 14.

Start small, get something working, and then gradually add features. Don't be afraid to look up documentation and examples.

# Final Thoughts

Lua's simplicity makes it approachable, but its unique features like first-class functions, flexible tables, powerful metatables, and lightweight coroutines provide remarkable depth and adaptability. It's a language that doesn't impose rigid structures but instead gives you versatile tools to build your own.

The path to mastery involves continued practice, exploration, and engagement. Build projects, read code written by others, participate in the community, and never stop being curious. The world of Lua is vast and rewarding.

www.ingramcontent.com/pod-product-compliance
Lightning Source LLC
LaVergne TN
LVHW081341050326
832903LV00024B/1251